THE
RIGHT,

THE
GOOD &

THE
HAPPY

OTHER BOOKS BY THE AUTHOR

Problems in Christian Apologetics
Protestant Biblical Interpretations
Protestant Christian Evidences
The Christian View of Science and Scripture
Varieties of Christian Apologetics
Special Revelation and the Word of God
A Handbook of Contemporary Theology
The Christian College in the Twentieth Century
The Pattern of Religious Authority
Them He Glorified

The Christian in a
World of Distorted Values

THE
RIGHT,
THE
GOOD &
THE
HAPPY

by

BERNARD L. RAMM

WORD BOOKS, PUBLISHER
Waco, Texas--London, England

THE RIGHT, THE GOOD AND THE HAPPY

Printed in the United States of America
Library of Congress Catalog Card Number: 70-144362

To the students of Baylor University

and the American Baptist Seminary of the West (Covina)

who have belabored these topics with me

in written form and oral discussion

and

To my son Stephen

who has had to live and learn many of these problems

as a university student and a member of the United States Navy

CONTENTS

PREFACE

This book is divided into two parts although that is not stated in the table of contents. The first three chapters deal with general ethical theory. The last two deal with very specific topics.

There is no universal law that states that a book is to be read from the first page to the last. If you are the typical "housewife" or "average man" or "man on the street" and have never read a line of ethics in your life, please don't start with chapter 1. Go directly to chapter 4 and start reading on specific subjects. Or look at the table of contents on chapters 4 and 5 and pick out the topics that interest you and read them.

Then if you become interested in the broader foundations of Christian ethics you can go back and read the first three chapters. But please don't get hung up on the first three chapters in order to get to the practical materials of the last two chapters. Hang loose on the way you read this book.

How this book is to be used:

In teaching ethics for many years the author has found that only a splinter of his students has had one course in philosophy. Furthermore, only a sliver of them has had a course in ethics. This book presumes *no* philosophical or ethical background for the reader.

Its intention is to introduce students in Christian schools to ethics, ethical problems, and forms of ethical argumentation. As much as possible it sets up the arguments for and against a given position. This is intended to teach the student to think in both directions in ethics. Not all the topics within this book are capable of that kind of treatment but this plan has been followed where it was possible. In some instances the author has set the issues down for the student to decide for himself; in others he has taken sides.

This is not a book arguing basic ethical theory. Many books on Christian ethics are very much preoccupied with this issue. Ian T. Ramsey, editor of *Christian Ethics and Contemporary Philosophy,* is completely occupied with the technical problems of ethics and philosophy. The intention of this book is very practical. It is based on the kinds of ethical problems the pastor will encounter and is an attempt to give *some* orientation for these problems.

As a text it may be used many ways. The pros and cons listed in the book can be the basis of class discussion. The omission of topics or arguments can suggest material for further lecturing to supplement the text. The topics which have been only briefly treated can be made assignments for research papers.

In short the intention of the book is instructional. It is not a handbook of solutions for all possible ethical problems which Christians face. Its purpose is to introduce students and pastors to ethical discourse and to get them *moving* in the direction of Christian ethics. Once on the move they can come into a period of their own maturation in Christian ethics.

We have intentionally limited our discussions to those kinds of issues which Christians may do something about. We have listed the reasons for a given position and the reasons against it. This is both to facilitate understanding of the ethical issue and provide the right kind of springboard for further discussion or research. We have kept the documentation to the absolute minimum on the basis that introductory works on a subject should be illuminating and explanatory rather than a showcase of scholarly research. All books mentioned in the text are fully documented in the Bibliography.

I

FOUNDATIONS IN CHRISTIAN ETHICS

Section 1: The Concept of Conduct

Theoretically every science should be able to indicate its special subject matter and the methodology that is peculiar to the science. In
ethics the subject matter is *conduct*.

This word is used in ethics in a special way for not all that man
does is *conduct* from an ethical point of view. A man may sneeze,
ransack the refrigerator, munch a cookie, or take his dog for a walk.
His activities are matters of taste, custom, or tradition. *Conduct* is
concerned with those actions that can be judged as right or wrong.
If a man sneezes, that is a neural reflex and not part of ethics. But if
a man tells a lie this act is right or wrong and therefore is classified
as *conduct*. In the most general sense the task of philosophical ethics
is to discover the principle or principles whereby an act of conduct can
be judged as right or wrong.

To some degree Christian ethics parallels the quest of philosophical
ethics. It too wishes to find the principle, principles, or policies of a
specific Christian nature that enable the Christian to assess the right-
ness or wrongness of a given case of conduct.

According to Christian ethics, however, *everything* that man does is
potentially conduct. Eating a sandwich is not a typical case of conduct,
but if a man gorges himself on sandwiches and gets sick, then eating
sandwiches is a matter of conduct. If the man persists in this habit
until he is grossly overweight with all the problems that creates, then
eating a sandwich is a matter of conduct. Whatever man does that is
ordinary, natural, or routine can be perverted, twisted, or overdone
and thereby become a matter of conduct.

Section 2: Ethics and Values

Ethics is not a study that stands by itself. Way back in Greek philosophy Plato saw that the *right,* the *good,* the *value,* and the *happy life* were different aspects of the same thing.

The *right* is the concern of ethics; the *good* is the quest for the highest of self-realization; the *value* is that which man cherishes; and the *happy life* is the kind of total existence all mankind wants. Christian ethics is also interested in the union and relatedness of these topics.

In the subsequent history of philosophy these issues were not always carefully sorted out. But beginning with the nineteenth century philosophers returned to the Platonic insight and began to treat specialized problems in ethics by expanding the coverage of topics within ethics. For example, value theory is now a whole study in itself with a large body of its own literature.

There is a good reason for looking at this cluster of the right, the good, and the valuable. It shows most of all the emptiness of a *pure moralism.* Ethics is not learning a rule or a principle or policy to follow in a given conduct situation. The right act is a good act, and the good should be part of the guide in choosing the right act. A right action brings with it a value, and what is of value should also be part of the stuff that goes into making an ethical decision. All three together have as their final goal the achievement of a satisfactory life on this earth.

This has real meaning for Christian ethics. The Christian ought to do the right thing, but Christian faith is not ethics and nothing more. It is concerned with man's total relationship to God and the character of the entire course of his life. The Christian is therefore also interested in the good, in the valuable, and in the happy life. For example, the Beatitudes are not a list of moral rules. They set forth the maxims of a *blessed* or *happy* life. Some translators do not follow the familiar "blessed is he" but substitute "happy is the man." The Beatitudes suggest more what is of value than what is morally right.

Since the time of deism and the moral philosophy of Kant there has been a steady force to reduce Christian faith to ethics, personal or social. But there is more to Christian faith than being moral or doing one's duty or obeying the commands of God. In other words, Christianity is not a moralism. In the Christian faith the right act is also the good act. The good act is also an experience of value.

In the discussions throughout this book the emphasis will be on ethics but this always implies that with the right something is being said about the good, about value, and about the happy life. The most basic assumption is that this unity grows out of the unity and harmony in the perfect nature of God from which also come the norms for the right, the good, and the valued.

Section 3: Ethical Theories

In philosophical ethics a large number of ethical theories have been defended. Most introductory books on ethics give summaries of these historical options or an entire book may be dedicated to explaining ethical systems as C. D. Broad's famous *Five Types of Ethical Theory*. We are concerned with the three of these theories which have to do with Christian ethics.

Deontological ethics. The word deontological is derived from a Greek word (*deon*) which carries the idea of the *ought* or the *binding*. Morality is doing one's duty, for what one ought to do is his duty to do. The truly moral man is one who can be counted on to be a man of principle and to always do his duty. It is therefore not uncommon in the history of Christian ethics to find the Christian norm stated in the form of an ethics of duty or of the ought.

It is perhaps impossible psychologically speaking to make an ethical decision with complete disregard of the consequences. Nevertheless a Christian ethic of duty theoretically ignores the consequences of the moral act, or at least minimizes them. Duty is duty regardless of the situation and regardless of the consequences. The consequences of moral decisions is God's business. If a man does his duty and it hurts another person or even leads to the death of an innocent person, the man is not to reckon with this. God's judgment will eventually even up the score. Many Jews died under Hitler because some Christians thought it their duty to tell the truth no matter what. When the Nazis asked them where the Jews were hiding they told them. These Christians felt that God would eventually give the Nazis their punishment.

Teleological ethic. The word teleological is derived from a Greek word meaning purpose or goal (*telos*). A moral decision is one in which the outcome or consequences or good produced is the criterion. The classic example of this kind of theory is the utilitarianism associ-

15

ated with such men as Bentham and Mill. The right decision is that decision which will produce the most good for the greatest number of people.

In Christian ethics this kind of theory is followed on the grounds that love expresses itself best this way, or that only a teleological ethic shows real regard for persons. It is further asserted that to act out of pure duty and to leave the consequences to God will result in very cruel treatment for many people.

Formal ethic. A formal ethic does not specify the content of an ethical act but the *necessary* form of any ethical act. The philosopher Kant is famous for his formal theory. His idea was that the principle in any moral decision was right if it could be universalized, and wrong if it couldn't. If a man is honest and all men are honest, a healthy society will be created. If a man cheats and all men cheat, society degenerates or becomes impossible.

In Christian ethics if love, and love alone, is set forth as the necessary form of a right act then we have a kind of formal ethics in Christianity. If one acts from love and love alone, a person does not necessarily know ahead of time what his specific action will be.

The problem with any formal theory of ethics is how to go from a purely formal (contentless) principle to a specific (content) ethical action.

Section 4: Act, Virtue, Character

As previously indicated ethics is not a subject by itself but involves value theory, theory of the good, and the happy life. The same qualifications must be made in another direction.

The *act* is the specific response to a specific ethical situation. It might be said to be the unit of conduct. To be ethical is to do the right act in each moral situation. In the mill of daily life we are not impressed, however, if some gangster contributes a very expensive floral display for his dead comrade and so helps adorn his funeral. Nor do we ordinarily consider a person morally corrupt because in one tight situation he tells a lie. Beyond act are *virtue* and *character*. A virtue is a settled moral attitude. If a man has the virtue of honesty he does not face each situation of cheating as a novel ethical situation. His settled virtue of honesty means that he will act true to form and not cheat. Ethics concerns not only the right act, but the *attitudes* or *principles* that make for right action which are deeply established in one's personality. A permanent policy or attitude is a virtue. Theologians of the Middle Ages worked out a veritable theology of virtue.

If a bad man does a good act we do not consider him by that act a good man. If a good man makes one bad decision we do not consider him as having become a degenerate person. We consider virtue or lack of virtue to be the real ethical character of people and judge them more by this criterion than by their singular acts.

Virtues produce character. A man may be honest in business but morally corrupt. A man has character when he has a sum or pattern of virtues. To act from character is to act from this sum of virtues. So a man of character is a man of many virtues, and we trust a man of character because he will act consistently from the sum of his virtues. A man without character is a man who has no established virtues. His actions cannot be trusted or predicted.

Christian ethics is interested in virtue and character because being a Christian is a total way of life. A total way of life for the Christian means the acquisition of many virtues. It is the life of a man of character, a man of God. In biblical language these virtues are called fruits of the Spirit (Gal. 5:22) and constitute the functioning principles of a man of character.

Ethics, especially Christian ethics, does not limit its vision to separate moral acts. Holy Scripture not only calls for the moral or right act, but for virtues which are established ethical patterns, and for character which demonstrates that the total man is a mature Christian and can therefore be trusted in all things. Again this means that scriptural ethics is not a pure moralism. It is not an ethic of isolated acts. Biblical ethics demands the richness and fulfillment of personality as expressed in the words "virtue" and "character." This idea is directly suggested in Hebrews 13:7 where the Christians are to note the *outcome* (Greek: *ekbasis,* "result of one's way of life") of the lives of their leaders. Christian ethics is as much interested in the *ekbasis* of one's life as it is in the character of individual moral acts.

Section 5: Biblical Religion and Ethics

Civilization is possible only because there are various laws, rules,

17

regulations, and ordinances. Calvin expressed this when he said there can be no society without discipline. Freud expressed it psychologically when he taught that every child must go through the process of socialization if he is to fit into society. We all know that no game from bridge to football is possible unless the rules are kept. Primitive societies that have no written documents nevertheless have elaborate codes which have been preserved through oral tradition.

The ancient Greeks were a reflective people. Their great philosophers asked the question: in the midst of all the rules, regulations, laws, customs, and traditions which bind a society together, are there any *exceptional* or *unusual* rules that are in a class by themselves? Are there some things we *ought* to do that make a demand or have an authority or a status different from all other social regulations?

Ethics began when some philosopher agreed that such rules existed and set out to find them. He sought for rules or principles which were more than customary, convenient, or regulatory and had the character of *ought* or *must* or *universality* about them. This oughtness, this must-do, and this universality are the attributes that differentiate an ethical statement from the ordinary rules of a society. Hence *philosophical ethics* was born.

This matter was not, however, left just to philosophers. Religion too felt that there were certain "oughts," "duties," or "commands" that were more than regulatory principles and that grew out of religious considerations. It is then possible to speak of a *religious ethics*. In this regard there is something very particular about the character of the ethics of Christianity or Holy Scripture which enables us to speak of *Christian ethics*.

Holy Scripture uses terms such as righteousness, holiness, and justice to describe the moral perfection of God. The God of the Old Testament and of the New Testament is a holy God, a moral God, and a righteous God. In the biblical God are not to be found the kinds of passions and immoral actions characteristic of the Greek gods. *In the biblical God there is no darkness.*

In turn this holy God requires that those who worship him must be holy people. The holiness of God's people is the ethical and moral character of their lives. In a profound sense freed from any notion of superficiality the believer in the God of Holy Scripture is to *imitate* this God. He is to love as God loves, be holy as God is holy, and be compassionate as God is compassionate. Only as he so imitates

God does the believer in the biblical God have a religious life which God honors. He is to love God, to serve God, to worship God, to adore God, to praise God, to commune with God, and to sing before God.

Holy Scripture is essentially a record of the love and goodness of God to man. God is a God of grace. He loves man in his sinnerhood. He pities him in his weakness. He is patient with man's rebellion against God. He makes the supreme sacrifice and sends his only Son to die for man. He pours out his Holy Spirit on the day of Pentecost that Christian man may have the power to lead the Christian life.

Yet he demands that man repent and turn from his wicked ways. He informs man that if he loves God he must love his fellow-man. He is told that if God is holy he must be holy; if God acts towards man in equity and justice, he must so act towards his fellow-man. If man believes in the moral character of God he will be moral towards his wife. If he thinks God is to be respected and honored he will teach this to his children.

Paul says very directly that people who think they are religious and yet persist in the things of the flesh—sins and their passions and their expressions—do not inherit the kingdom of God (Gal. 5:16–21). A holy God honors holy people. The people who worship the Lord must imitate the Lord's moral nature. Biblical religion without ethics is a contradiction. The worship of the living God before an altar or in a temple demands from the worshiper maximum ethical concern.

Section 6: Practical Religion

Primitive man's science is his magic. By his magic he sought to control his universe so as to avoid the evil, experience the good, and cure the sick. This is religion at its *animistic* level. This is the belief that man's world is populated with evil and good spirits with which man is fighting for or with all the days of his life. This is *practical* religion in its worst sense and stands in radical contrast to Christian revelation.

Primitive man follows a religion in order to insure *practical* results. He wants to catch fish, trap game, grow crops, avoid a curse, kill an enemy, or heal the sick. In being so *practically* oriented morality or ethics in a reflective or philosophical sense does not exist. Animism is basically amoral—a religion without a morality. It has divorced holiness from its spirits, follows religious practices with no moral elements, and represents the religious man as a man without character, spirituality, or moral dignity.

Biblical religion is also interested in the practical. But this practicality (concern for specific goods and avoidance of specific evils) is never divorced from the holiness of the God of biblical revelation. Whatever the biblical man does of a practical nature, or whenever he prays to his God about a practical matter, it is always within the context of a religion that demands from him a genuine moral life.

It is perhaps an overstatement to say that there are no genuine ethical elements in animistic and polytheistic religions. Part of the uniqueness of Socrates was to purify the Greeks' ideas of their gods and their religion (as seen in Xenophon's life of Socrates, *The Memorabilia,* and the Platonic dialogue on piety, *The Euthyphro*). But in general ethical concern is at a minimum and there is no vision of the intimate connection of religion with ethics. The emphasis falls more on cult worship and the concern for practical results from religion.

It has been said that the genius of biblical religion is that it has affirmed that true religion requires worshipers with maximum ethical and moral concerns. This is not the unique element in biblical revelation, but it is certainly a clear witness to the fact that *practicality* or *relevance* in the biblical religion is always within the context of the moral and the ethical. A cardinal sin according to Holy Scripture is to refuse to recognize the essential principle that a holy God requires holiness in those who serve him.

Section 7: Man, Incurably Moral

A freshman is not in a university very long before he learns that there is no universal moral code by which all the nations of the earth live. He discovers that there are as many ethical systems as there are tribes or peoples or nations or cultures. He may conclude that all ethical systems are relative, culturally conditioned, and lack universality.

In some cultures human beings have been sacrificed to the gods. In America the sacrifice of a person in a religious ritual is murder. In another culture a wife feels neglected and unloved if her husband does

20

not periodically beat her; in England this would be considered brutality. It was common for the Romans to let unwanted children die by deserting them; in America a hundred thousand dollars may be spent to preserve the life of one very sick child.

Henry Sidgwick (1838-1900) was one of England's most famous ethicists. His work *Methods of Ethics* (1874) was a standard textbook in British schools for years. According to him all men are bound by the duties given man from God. Variations to these rules by other cultures were the results of their ignorance. The different cultural and ethical patterns of the African or Asiatic nations were no challenge to universal moral law.

One of Sidgwick's students, Edward Westermarck, had a different theory. Variations in ethics could not be settled by an appeal to ignorance. There are no universal moral laws. In reality there are customs or habits or rules or mores that each society has to maintain its life. The way of prudence in ethics is to conform with one's society if for no other reason than it saves one from all the difficulties that go with bucking the traditions of a society.

There is valuable insight in both opinions. Westermarck was right in that empirically speaking it cannot be demonstrated that one set of universal ethical principles is found around the world. Rather, anthropologists have found endless variations. In this sense all ethical systems are relative to their particular culture.

Sidgwick was right in that man cannot be amoral or nonethical. Wherever man is found he does have some rules, some principles, some oughts, some regulations. Human existence apart from some sort of commonly accepted regulations is impossible. In this sense there is universal moral consciousness.

Conflicting lists of rights and wrongs do not prove that man is an amoral creature. They do illustrate the enormous diversity of rights and wrongs in divergent cultures. But man is incurably ethical and incurably moral because in every culture *some* things are right, and *some* things are wrong. Each culture treats these not just as customs or mere traditions but as having some kind of moral force, some kind of absolute character expressed in modern ethical language by the word *ought.*

There is some verification of this in psychiatry. Freud said that all men except the psychopath have a superego. By superego he meant the sum of all the "don'ts" imposed upon a child by his parents, teachers, and other elders. This helps form the "socialization" of man, i.e., man learns how to live with his fellow-man. It is but the psychiatric synonym for conscience. Furthermore, all people have guilt feelings. Much of the work of the psychiatrist is to help people shake off false guilt feelings. It has been said that the greatest foe of the psychiatrist is the feeling of guilt because it is so hard for people to feel forgiven. Although this is pathologically induced guilt and not guilt based on acts that are sinful acts, it is still a witness to the fact that man is incurably ethical.

The Christian position is that one must make a distinction between divergent ethical systems and the universally experienced phenomenon of the *ought*. Man is incurably moral not in the sense that all cultures have the same ethical principles but that in all cultures there are moral systems; there are rights and wrongs; there is the universal experience of the *ought*.

Section 8: Ethics Based on Religion

One of the strongest convictions of philosophers in the past one hundred years is that ethics can be discussed independently from religion. The traditional notion of the Western Christian heritage that ethics grows out of religion is strongly repudiated. Ethics can be developed from reason, or intuition, or experience, or analysis. There is no need for recourse to religion for the foundations, principles, or sanctions of ethics.

This view is not held only by philosophers. There are Christian ethicists who believe that the experience of the ethical is unique and universal and may be developed independently from religion or theology. As Christians they will add Christian elements to their ethical system as a necessary addition to a purely philosophical ethic.

(1) This view is argued on the basis that ethics is autonomous, a kind of phenomenon or human behavior that can be investigated independently from religious considerations. To put it another way, ethics can be broken off from religion and treated as an autonomous discipline.

(2) Or, it is argued that the good is *intrinsically* good. We do not need God or religion to make the good good. If a moral principle is good, it is good in itself and therefore does not need to be propped up

22

by God nor religion. This is justification for separating ethics from religion.

Historically the theologians in the Christian church have thought otherwise. God's will *includes* the ethical. The Christian doctrine of sanctification and the Christian life have large ethical elements in them. Christian theology provides the sanctions (the important reasons for) for ethics. Holy Scripture has dozens of ethical exhortations in it. In biblical religion or Christianity ethics and theology cannot be separated.

The Christian theologian may attack the theory that ethics is free from religion from three perspectives:

(1) Man as a sinner can know the good and the right only by divine revelation. As long as the matter is kept in the abstract or theoretical it may appear as if ethics and theology can be developed independently. But when concrete goods, rights, and values are discussed the Christian theologian believes that these *specifics* can be settled only by reference to divine revelation.

(2) From the standpoint of the Christian doctrine of God, God is a *good* God. God's commands are *good* commands. To speak as if *good* were intrinsic and needed no reference to God is to deny that God is a good God. It is to create a false and contradictory problem. A good God reveals to man those ethical principles that are good. The good is good because it comes from a good God, and a good God orders and decrees only the good. From this standpoint Christian ethics grows out of the goodness in God and therefore ethics cannot be separated from theology.

(3) From the standpoint of Christian theology ethics is part of a larger system and cannot be broken off from it. A holy God, as indicated, must be worshiped in ethical integrity; ethical sanctions rest upon God as the Lord of every man; ethical motivation and strength come from the doctrine of the Holy Spirit. The good, the right, the value, and the truth are all understood by the Christian by means of divine revelation and find themselves ultimately imbedded in the character of a glorious and perfect God.

If ethics is not only doing one's duty but involves rewards and punishments, the balancing of the books when life is over, then again ethics is dependent upon theology. It is a fact that philosophers who ignore divine revelation do discuss ethics. Men who are not Christians do write books on ethics. But from the standpoint of Christian theology, ethics is a segment *within* the whole context of the Christian faith and is abstract or devoid of force and motivation if removed from its locus in Christian theology.

Karl Barth has made a strong attack upon the idea that ethics can be separated from theology. First, man as sinner does not know the command of God. He can learn it only through revelation. Second, the separation of ethics from theology is but another version of the analogy of being or natural theology (i.e., that man can come to some truth about God by pure reason without the help of grace or revelation), and natural theology is classified by Barth as next to the Antichrist. Third, the practice of breaking ethics away from theology in theological faculties and seminaries and making special courses in ethics or special departments of ethics is to deny the moral nature and moral integrity of God. In a radical move Barth makes fundamental theory of ethics part of the doctrine of God; otherwise one could have a God who was by implication amoral. Unfortunately Barth discusses ethics in so many places in his *Church Dogmatics* with such long exposition it is very difficult to set down his ethics. His theological basis which is primary for all his ethical thought will be found in *Church Dogmatics,* II/2.

Section 9: Man As the Moral Agent in Christian Ethics

Christians ethics presumes among other things a definite view of man, for it is man that is morally related to God. The major elements of the biblical doctrine of man as they apply to Christian ethics are:

(1) Man is God's special creation. Man lives in his world responsible to the God who created it; he lives with his fellow-man and is especially responsible to him since he too is God's special creation; man is responsible to God for the manner in which he uses God's creation and in which he treats his own person. Man's moral life is not a series of separate encounters but it is lived out in the total relationships of creation.

He is also specially created by God to be a moral person. He has *intelligence* so that he can perceive an ethical situation, understand the matter of decision, and anticipate the consequences of his action. He has *emotion* so that when he makes his ethical decisions, right or wrong, he *feels* a certain way about his actions. He has a *moral ele-*

ment imbedded in his nature so that he is not pure intellect, nor are his actions pure spontaneity like those of an animal. This moral element in man is usually called conscience.

Some have thought of conscience as a separate faculty in man's nature by which he assesses the moral elements in his experience. Others have looked upon conscience as part of the general composition of man, but that part which is aware of the moral dimension of human experience.

It is a maxim that conscience should be our guide, yet at the same time we know that conscience is not a uniform quantity in each man but varies enormously from person to person as expressed in such phrases as "a hardened conscience," "a dead conscience," or "a tender conscience." The paradox is, then, that man as a moral creature is to guide his way through life by conscience, yet knowing all the time the fallibility of conscience.

Claude A. Pierce attempted to give a new interpretation of conscience in his work, *Conscience in the New Testament*. The basic thesis is that conscience is the way in which man reacts to his moral decisions. If he lives up to his ideals he feels positive emotional reenforcement; if he strays from his ideals he has guilt feelings. He makes his moral decisions by intelligence morally informed. Although this is a carefully reasoned argument by Pierce, it has not as yet won universal acceptance and is at variance with some of the verses about conscience in the New Testament. Pragmatically speaking there is little difference between the older view of conscience and Pierce's view because it is the same furniture shifted around.

The Christian addition to the ordinary doctrine of conscience is that it is located in the total range of Christian experience and teaching. That is to say a Christian conscience is informed by the moral teaching of Scripture and is made sensitive by the indwelling Spirit of God.

Man is God's creature and as such he is *covenantly* related to God. The concept of covenant as that which binds man and God together is a major Old Testament theme. It pertains not only to God and individual man but also to God and Israel. In the New Testament period the covenant binds God and the church. Man's moral actions occur within this covenantal relationship which is spelled out in precise terms.

(2) Man is a sinner. Moral philosophers did not ignore that man could be the victim of his passions. There is Plato's image in which

25

one horse is pulling man heavenward and the other earthward. But the Christian faith puts an emphasis on waywardness not usually found in philosophical ethics, although Kant came close to it with his ideas of the "Bad Principle" and the "Radical Evil" in human nature.

Kant also said that if a man ought, he can. This goes contrary to the Christian doctrine of sin. The most relevant passage at this point is Romans 7 where Paul makes painfully clear that what he *ought* to do he *can't*. It must be admitted that most philosophers agree with Kant and not with Paul.

According to Holy Scripture man is ethically darkened, ethically weak, and ethically corrupt. He desperately needs light, strength, and purification. Therefore in the New Testament the foundation of moral living is redemption for only in redemption is there a measure of cure for the crippling effects of sin.

As far as the knowledge of the right is concerned, man as sinner is in need of special revelation. The source of special revelation and the foundation for basic knowledge and doctrine of Christian ethics is Holy Scripture. Certainly not every ethical issue can be settled by pinpoint reference to Scripture, but where Scripture does not contain specifics it at least indicates some of the ways we ought to think in resolving our contemporary ethical problems.

It is for these reasons (man's sin and God's special revelation) that Barth and Brunner stress the priority of the command of God in their ethical theory. This is not to set forth a legalistic ethics, nor an ethics that ignores persons and situations to favor sheer obedience to principles. The point is that God is Lord, he is the supreme moral person, and in any conflict between the Lord God and man, the command of God has priority.

The Christian insists that a good God issues only good commands. The Christian wants mercy to triumph over justice. He does not want an ethics that is moralistic and legalistic. But the Christian does not forget the doctrine of sin. Man and God are in conflict. This conflict can break out in ethics as well as in other places. In this conflict the Christian places the priority of the command of God above the opinions of men. Because Barth wrote so ponderously and obscurely it was not really known that he defended situation ethics long before Fletcher. But Barth is still solidly enough in the biblical tradition to know that in any conflict of God and man over an ethical issue the command of God has priority.

(3) The Christian man is a man in grace. Christian man is redeemed, pardoned, justified, and regenerated. This is the platform on which he can build an ethical life. The past is erased through the forgiveness of sins and justification. New life and power is made possible by the new birth and the indwelling Spirit of God.

The Christian man as a man in grace is also a man who has a real foundation for treating the problem of *motivation*. For example, students today are exposed to much information and lecturing about the evils of drugs, venereal diseases, and alcohol, but the impact of this in terms of changed conduct is very small. Information about the evils of drugs is not the same as motivation to change one's habits. One of the weakest elements in philosophical ethics is motivation. There are some very brilliant analyses of what the right is, or the nature of the good, or the logical form of an ethical sentence. But somehow the matter of motivation is skipped or if treated it comes through rather weakly.

For the Christian the problem of motivation is one of the most important parts of ethics. Why do the right? Why seek the good? Why flee the evil?

There is a clash here between the Platonic view of motivation and the Christian view. According to Plato if a man *saw* or *knew* the truth he would do it. Ignorance or lack of comprehension was at the root of all waywardness. On the superficial level Plato was certainly wrong. Most people who break laws, or in theological language who sin, know ahead of time what they are about to do. Robbers, liars, embezzlers, and blackmailers are not acting out of ignorance. The old Roman maxim is true: we know the good but do the evil.

Plato can be defended on only one assumption. To *know* means to know in fullest depth what an action involves. If a man knew the whole range of his action from original motivation to final consequences, *then* he would do the truth. *Then* ignorance is not some simple thing like not knowing that stealing is wrong but a failure to know the entire dimensions of an ethical act. There is perhaps much truth in this interpretation of Plato. But if man is depraved he still could have this depth knowledge of ethical action and sin and not act on it. Furthermore, only a very few members of the human race could ever achieve Plato's kind of ethical comprehension.

Man in grace is different. The experience of conviction by the Spirit and repentance from sin has shown man the evil of his former

27

way of life. The message of grace in the gospel has opened his eyes and heart to the love of God. The sacrifice of Christ on the cross arouses within him a profound sense of gratitude. He sees his old life ended at the cross and a new life beginning at the resurrection (Rom. 6). He is now no longer a debtor to sin but a captive to grace in which he is led, guided, inspired, and empowered by the Holy Spirit. Faith is not only trust in Christ but obedience to Christ. Finally he knows that he must make his final reckoning with Christ his Lord (1 Cor. 3:12–15, 2 Cor. 5:10, Rom. 14:10–12).

This does not insure perfection of motivation in the Christian nor is it a shield against false motivation and lapses from the Christian way of life. But there is a power of motivation for the right in the Christian faith that is absent in philosophical ethics.

(4) The Christian man is a moral man within a qualified freedom. Such a statement that man is a "free moral agent" is an oversimplification. Freedom is a presupposition for ethical experience. Determinism or freedom can be discussed only on the presupposition of freedom. To argue for determinism makes sense only if the reader has the freedom to assess the truth of the arguments. Efforts to argue for determinism—philosophical, psychological, or theological—all have this inner contradiction built into them.

Responsibility for one's actions and liability to judgment for sin or crime presumes a measure of freedom in man. But this is a *qualified* freedom.

(i) Every person in a moral situation brings his entire self to the decision. All his previous experiences are factors in the ethical situation. He does not come as if he had no prejudices, no convictions, no learning from the past. He does not enter an ethical situation on the principle of "equal indifference" as if his choice were like flipping a coin. He has freedom but a freedom qualified by the totality of his past experiences.

(ii) Every person engages in some rationalization. To rationalize means to give supposedly good reasons for an act that really has no such reasons. If a man finds himself pulled in the wrong direction through temptation, he soon finds himself making up reasons for the wrong decision. To be human is to rationalize. Therefore any concept of freedom in ethical decision must be seen in the context of the universal propensity of man to rationalize his bad actions in order to make them appear just. We are all guilty of the *specious* argument—

that argument which looks so rational when set forth but comes apart when subjected to critical analysis.

(iii) Man acts compulsively and the concept of freedom in morality must be seen in this perspective. To act compulsively is to act according to a motivation that is repressed below the level of consciousness and yet is a powerful force in shaping our decisions. A person may think he does something for one reason but he really does it compulsively for another reason.

Hypnosis supplies a good illustration of this. While in a hypnotic state a person is told upon returning to normal consciousness he will close an open window. When brought out of hypnosis he does close the window. When asked why he closed the window he starts to give reasons about drafts, colds, or chills. Yet the audience knows that the real motivation was the instruction given the man through hypnosis.

A person may be driven by suppressed guilt from past immoral actions. He atones for this guilt by being a perfect clerk or salesman or church member. On the surface he says he does these things because a responsible person ought to conduct himself this way. But the real motivation is the suppressed feeling of guilt. Therefore any concept of man as a "free moral agent" must be corrected by what we know of man's unconscious compulsive motivation.

Section 10: Sanctions

A motive is an inner reason for an outward action. The Christian may be motivated to right action by his love and gratitude to Christ for dying for him. A sanction is a reason for acting the right ethical way in view of the consequences of one's acts. Hence sanctions have sometimes been called the *external* reasons for right moral action.

In the history of philosophy sanctions have usually been associated with the outcome of an ethical life. *If* a man follows the right and the good he will lead a happy life or a good life. *If* a man persists in being a criminal then his life becomes one wretched game of seeking escape from the police and never knowing the joy and tranquility of a normal home existence. The moral issue is then never simply to do the right or the wrong, to be ethical or unethical. But over every life hang sanctions. Wrong decisions have unhappy consequences; right decisions lead to a life of peace or contentment or satisfaction.

The Christian ethic also has its sanctions and certainly accepts what the philosophical ethicists have said about the outcome in this life of one's moral or immoral acts. However, it uses some different words. The Christian ethic speaks of *blessings* and *cursings*. Deuteronomy 27 speaks line after line of the cursings that come to the man who violates the law, whereas chapter 28 speaks of the blessings that come to the man who keeps the law. In Matthew 5:3-11, Christ speaks of the blessedness of the man who keeps the ethics of the kingdom of God. The cursedness of the man who doesn't is reported in Matthew 7:24-27.

Psalm 1 is a model on the theme of sanctions: "The wicked are not so, but are like chaff which the wind drives away. Therefore the wicked will not stand in the judgment, nor sinners in the congregation of the righteous; for the Lord knows the way of the righteous, but the way of the wicked will perish" (vv. 4-6).

Holy Scripture also speaks of sanctions in terms of punishments and rewards. This has been attacked as acting morally only for the fact that man avoids pain or seeks some extra approval. He is like a child who obeys his mother for the stick of candy he will get for his obedience and not because he really honors his mother. No doubt some unfortunate preaching may give this impression.

This is, however, not to have the picture in focus. We have seen in several instances already that man is not pure moral agent and that the moral life is not simply a series of right ethical decisions. Man as moral man, man as ethical man, *is man with a destiny. Destiny* means that the total character of a man's life has an outcome. Just as ethical act cannot be divorced from character neither can it be divorced from destiny. Consistent moral behavior produces virtues and virtues produce character, *a total life character.* This is expressed in the ideas of rewards and punishments. The sanction is this: *one's whole life is on the line in the manner in which he lives and therefore ends in a total decision of judgment or salvation.* Therefore in Christian ethics sanctions are never an academic question. Christian ethics is not composed only of moral principles, or a simple desire to live one way and not another. The biblical doctrine of sanctions shows the absolute seriousness of the morality and ethical character of the total man in view of his life-and-death probationary status on this earth.

Section 11: The Use of Scripture in Christian Ethics

The Christian accepts Holy Scripture as his final appeal in matters of faith and practice and this means that to be consistent he must apply this decision to ethics. It is impossible, however, for Scripture to speak on all possible moral situations. Problems of an ethical nature which have never heretofore existed face us in the twentieth century. The Christian wants a biblical ethics; he wants to be faithful to the divine revelation. But this ideal is difficult to achieve.

The Christian interpreter of Scripture must decide what the biblical teaching on a moral issue is. He is faced with several hurdles. Holy Scripture is a large book with more than a thousand pages in most editions. That is a lot of material to go through and sort out before one can arrive at the biblical position on a given point. Further, Holy Scripture is divided into two testaments, and the second or the New Testament tells us that much in the Old Testament is not binding on the church. But some of it is. The ethicist must sort out what in the Old Testament carries over to the church and what is outdated.

Much of what Holy Scripture teaches is bound to a historic period and to an alien culture. Since biblical times hundreds of other items have entered into human culture. In such a complicated set of circumstances what can be meant by a biblical ethic?

(1) One solution to the problem outlined is to appeal to the church. The theology of the Roman Catholic church teaches that the church functions as a teaching magisterium. Some of its pronouncements are infallible (the *ex cathedra* statements of the pope, and the decrees of an ecumenical council). Others are authoritative or binding without being infallible such as the papal encyclicals. The teaching magisterium of the church further has a special grace which enables it to understand the meaning of Scripture. The Roman Catholic layman is able to obtain proper ethical advice from the teaching magisterium of the church which mediates the biblical revelation and tradition for the modern moral problem. A number of papal encyclicals have been concerned with social issues and have pioneered in thought beyond the Protestants (*Rerum Novarum, Quadragesimo Anno, Divini Redemptoris, Mater et Magistra, Pacem in Terris*).

To resort to the church to find the right ethical decision for modern man is not without its problems. Facts cannot be compelled. Today scholars determine the meaning of words or phrases or expressions

31

by resorting to an elaborate scholarly apparatus previous scholars did not have. The church cannot simply set forth its decisions regardless of this scholarship but must come to terms with it. This makes it very difficult for the pope to utter some decree or encyclical and have it accepted by the scholars simply because he, the pope, said it. For the scholar, just to announce the meaning of a passage of Scripture is not acceptable. To him the decisions of the pope are purely arbitrary if not built on scholarly foundations.

There is an element of the church solution in Paul Lehmann's *Ethics in a Christian Context*. At some points his contextual ethics is similar to situation ethics and at other points it differs. A significant element in forming an ethical judgment, according to Lehmann, is the Christian community. This community gathered in the name of Jesus Christ is part of the context or situation within which a decision is made. The church may even be thought of as an ethical laboratory, a fellowship, in which Christians attempt to come to ethical maturity. This is certainly a commendable effort to relate personal decision in ethics to the mind of the total Christian community without the problems found in the Roman Catholic theory of the church solution.

Lehmann's idea is a good corrective for another problem. In the concrete existence of the local church the ethics of the church tend to be the ethics of the pastor who does most of the preaching and teaching in the church. Lehmann's theory of ethics makes the task of finding the mind of Christ the task of the whole community and not the sole responsibility of the preacher. This is not to rob the pastor of his prophetic role, but it does prevent an unfortunate individualism. Seeking the mind of Christ and the leading of the Spirit in the whole church keeps things in balance.

(2) Another way in which a Christian may attempt to find the will of God in Scripture on an ethical point is to consider that all of Scripture in every way is the Word of God. All of Scripture, directly or indirectly, in plain teaching or in narrative, bristles with moral directives. There are potential ethical maxims lurking everywhere in Scripture, even in the most commonplace passage. Christian conscience is bound not only to the clear ethical statements of Scripture but also to all the maxims of Scripture which can be decoded from a dozen different incidents.

(i) The first problem with such a use of the Bible for ethical direction is that it fails to see the progress of revelation in the historical

32

development of Scripture. A truth gleaned from some event in Judges binds the conscience as much for these people as Romans 8, for the Word of God is one, and all parts that express God's will have equal authority. Such a treatment of Scripture not only violates the progressive character which the Scripture itself teaches but makes Christian ethics arbitrary.

(ii) Another problem involved with this viewpoint is that it tends to put more weight for ethical decision on the Old Testament than the New. For example, it gives the Ten Commandments a status of priority not actually found in the Scriptures themselves. Whenever such people talk of natural law they speak of the Ten Commandments and not the Sermon on the Mount or the ethical teachings of Paul. Because the Old Testament is so large and full of historical incidents, there is an imbalance in ethics based on this belief. Ethical maxims are drawn from the rich historical materials of the Old Testament and the more direct ethical teachings of the New Testament are neglected.

(iii) In the attempt to be loyal to the Word of God and bend the will of man to the truth of God those who follow this use of Scripture unintentionally work a hardship on some and cruelty on others. A Christian is to obey the moral teaching of Scripture "no matter what." And that "no matter what" can entail some very bitter experiences and some lonely sufferings. The uniqueness of the person and the special character of the situation are necessary ingredients in any fair ethical decision, but this use of Scripture runs persons and situations into the ground in the devout but mistaken effort to uphold the divine authority of Scripture.

(iv) This use of Scripture leads to some odd arguments for ethical principles. It attempts to judge the moral issue of birth control from the actions of Onan. Or it attempts to defend a political theory by appealing to the political structures of the Old Testament. Or it takes the various rules of Leviticus and Deuteronomy and attempts to settle moral issues of the modern age from customs or practices of an ancient culture.

The basic cure for this mistaken attempt to glean ethical principles from Scripture is to grant the priority of the New Testament in all matters of ethics. The New Testament is the ethical center of gravity in Holy Scripture. Whatever is said in the Old Testament must be evaluated from the perspective of the New Testament.

We have spent some space with this theory of the use of Scriptures for Christian ethics because it is so popular and leads to many defective judgments in ethical matters.

(3) Another method of discerning real ethical content from Scripture is to resort to a Christological interpretation of Scripture. Such a position includes within itself the priority of the New Testament over the Old. But it attempts to make it a more systematic and usable principle. The person of Christ is the perfect man before God. The emphasis is not so much that he lived the perfect life (a principal concept found in older works), but that he reflected the right kind of values, the right nature of the good, the right attitudes toward all classes of people, and preeminently the way of love in all ethical confrontations. By using such a Christological criterion, ethical statements of the Old Testament as well as incidents with proposed ethical content are not accepted at face value. If they contradict the ethics suggested by the whole life of the Son of God, they are not binding on Christians. That part of the Old Testament which can be binding to Christians must pass the Christological test. At least if it is not directly Christological in content, it may not contradict what we know about Christ. This kind of Christological use of the Scripture is supposedly derived from Luther and is much in vogue with neoorthodox theologians.

The first advantage of this position is that it does represent a cure for many of the historical abuses of Holy Scripture. A Christological ethic will be more humane, more tolerant, and more considerate of persons and situations than older systems which tended to be legalistic and really failed to give each person and each situation its proper weight in arriving at the right decision.

Christian ethics has always affirmed that in Jesus Christ, whose teaching was sanctioned by the one perfect, sinless life, we have the supreme ethical teacher of the human race. Therefore the New Testament makes constant appeal to the moral perfection of Jesus as the example for Christians (1 Pet. 2:21, 1 John 3:16, Heb. 12:3, Phil. 2:5, Rom. 8:29, 1 Cor. 15:49, 2 Cor. 3:18, 2 Cor. 8:9, Acts 20:35, and Col. 3:10).

Such a Christological ethic is an improvement over the sentimentality of the "do-as-Jesus-would" ethic of a previous liberal generation. It is a healthy and solid corrective to the superficial Protestant idea of the imitation of Jesus. This older "do-as-Jesus-would" ethic had the right idea but it was too amateurish and theologically naïve to be the permanent basis for Christian ethics.

However, a Christological ethic taken without any significant modification creates two problems: (i) How could a man of God in the Old Testament know how to sort out his ethical decisions if he had no knowledge of Jesus Christ? (ii) Treating the moral content of the Old Testament by testing by "the spirit of Jesus" is not new with neoorthodoxy. It was part of the basic ethical theory of the older religious liberalism. And it creates a problem that the neoorthodox must also reckon with. Namely, *which Jesus are you referring to?*

The liberals of yesteryears felt quite free to reject all sorts of things that Jesus said especially about hell and damnation. When they tested the Old Testament by "the spirit of Jesus" it was a Jesus they had fashioned out of their own imagination. The Jesus of this ethical principle turns out to be a contemporary religious liberal projected backwards into the first Christian century.

A Christological ethic must be built from the Christ of the total witness of the New Testament. A Jesus cut down to our likings and our presuppositions and our sentimentalities is not the Jesus of the New Testament. The liberals failed at this point. Neoorthodoxy at times comes very close to imitating this older heresy and in certain passages in Brunner it is not a danger but an actual trespass. The Jesus Christ of a Christological ethic should be no more a neoorthodox Jesus than a liberal Jesus. He can only be the Jesus of the whole of the New Testament.

(4) Another way of looking at Holy Scripture as a source of Christian ethics is to recognize from the very first that it does not intend to give direction for every conceivable moral situation. Indeed with the advance of culture it could not. Any person who has carefully gone through the New Testament for its proposed ethical system, or has read attempts to summarize New Testament ethics (Dewar, Schnackenburg, Feine) has discovered that the ethical teaching of the New Testament yields to no system. It is incomplete at some points and has nothing to say at other places where it is felt something should be said. For example, Paul wrote that "it is better to marry than to be aflame with passion" (1 Cor. 7:9 RSV). But what is the Christian to say to people who are sexually aflame with passion and where marriage is not a possibility for some reason or other? Paul is silent at this point. Or, if the teachings about wealth by Jesus are compared with those of Paul we do not find contradiction but certainly different rules for handling one's wealth as a Christian. Compare for example the advice given to the rich man by Jesus in Luke 18:18–30 ("sell all"), and how

Paul advises wealthy Christians not to sell all but to use their wealth in Christian stewardship (1 Tim. 6:17–19).

The right way to approach Holy Scripture as a guide for Christian ethics is not to see it as a total handbook or an exhaustive dictionary of Christian ethics. The Bible does contain examples of the right kinds of moral decisions, the standards God expects of us, the sort of policies or attitudes we are to have, and patterns or models for our ethical decisions. Holy Scripture gives us clues to the kind of moral and ethical thinking which is pleasing to God. By following this procedure we gain not only the specifics which Scripture teaches, but we gain policies so that we can come to a Christian understanding of those ethical situations not treated in Scripture.

Narcotics are not mentioned in Scripture but certainly what Scripture says of strong drink and of the body as the temple of the Holy Ghost will give us some guidance on this subject. It seems that if one takes Scripture as containing essentially a formal, theological system of ethics the only way in which such an ethics could be obeyed is to recreate the cultural backdrop of the New Testament and Old Testament periods. But even here we run into a problem because there are several cultures represented in Scripture out of which moral teaching came.

If we look at Scripture as giving us not only specifics but how to think ethically, how to surmise the mind of God on those things not expressed in Scripture, then Scripture can be a living guide for all generations and all cultures speaking a relevant word wherever it is read and whenever it is read.

II

TRADITIONAL CHRISTIAN NORMS

Section 100: Natural Law

There are some standards or rules or norms that appear as constants in the history of Christian ethics. In this chapter we shall attempt to give just the essence of these constants which in some instances are shared by philosophers, Jews, Roman Catholics, and Protestants.

The concept of natural law is the most uniform constant in the history of ethics. It was propounded by the Greeks, accepted by the Christians, modified one way or the other by the Reformers, and even today is part of the basis of law in countries that do not profess Christianity. Because it is a concept believed by such divergent groups, and over such a long period of time, it is a concept that comes in many versions. It has also come under serious criticism from both philosophers and theologians on the grounds that no such concrete or realistic or practical law exists. But since it is the most universal ethical principle, it must be given at least a summary treatment.

(1) The Greek version stems mainly from the Stoics. There is a universal reason in all things. It was the Stoics who first developed the philosophical notion of the *logos* or *logoi* (plural), namely, that all of nature is permeated by and controlled by principles of reason. Part of universal reason is the moral nature of man. It may be expressed as natural law. Experience and reflection will enable the philosopher to identify these natural laws.

(2) The concept of natural law was taken over by Roman Catholic theologians. It received particular attention by Thomas Aquinas. The Roman Catholic view is that the moral law of God is built into creation and therefore into man and is the universal moral law for the

37

human race. It applies to Christians and non-Christians alike. For example, the idea that procreation is the purpose of human sexuality is derived from natural law. What is natural law can be applied to all men. So the Roman Catholic church feels free to have legislation enacted that prohibits birth control not on the specific grounds that it is a matter of conscience with Roman Catholics, but that it is natural law. As natural law it applies to all men.

There is a hard line and a soft line about natural law in Roman Catholic moral theology. The hard line tries to keep the Thomistic and medieval view as the official view of natural law. The soft line is taken by Roman Catholics who realize some of the problems set out by philosophers and anthropologists in isolating specifics of natural law and of the problem of so many variant ethical systems in the world.

The hard line is set forth in the Roman Catholic *Dictionary of Moral Theology* ("Law, natural"). "Natural law is universal, immutable, not dispensable, and perceptible. It applies everywhere and for all men; it cannot change with the passage of time; no one can dispense from its observance; it may be understood or perceived by anyone who attains the use of reason; its observance obliges when it is perceived by a person who has the use of reason" (p. 697).

(3) It is difficult to speak of a Protestant version but more of Protestant versions. Some base natural law on man's creation. Being made in the image of God he must have impressed upon his mind a set of moral concepts. Others look at the Ten Commandments as not only projecting forward the kind of ethical life expected of Israel but as a recovery of the natural law originally given to Adam. Others look at natural law not as so many specifics but as kinds of general rules like rules of good health. By experience and reason man learns if he does certain things he gets into trouble and if he does other things life goes better. The great divergence in ethical systems is not so divergent as it seems. For example, the diets of people vary greatly but they are still within limits or people would not survive. So divergent ethical systems are always within limits and man has society only as he lives within these rather elastic limits. Accordingly it is argued that unless one agrees to some kind of natural law he is driven to a destructive ethical relativism or even to amoral nihilism.

The core of the major objections to natural law is that it simply cannot handle such wide divergences of ethical belief. Or stated another way, it defaults in that it cannot really get down to specifics in a conclusive way.

This is a brief summary of the issues about a very complex topic, but it is intended only to suggest what the concept is, who has defended it and why, and why it has been subject to searching criticism especially since the advent of modern philosophy (e.g., Hobbes, Grotius).

Section 101: The Ten Commandments

There is no question that the Ten Commandments (Jewish tradition, The Ten Words) have exerted more influence on ethics and law in Christian countries than any other part of Scripture or any document outside of Scripture.

In Roman Catholic moral theology, in Protestant ethics, and in Western law the Ten Commandments has been the fundamental document. It was not unusual for legal codes of the Middle Ages to be prefaced with the Ten Commandments. Part of medieval piety was to write commentaries on the Ten Commandments which the Reformers also did (Luther, *Larger Catechism* and *Treatise on Good Works*; Calvin, *Institutes of the Christian Religion*, II, 8).

There are two listings of the Ten Commandments (Exod. 20:1–17, Deut. 5:6–21). This is not unusual nor are the variations unusual, as it was customary in those days to repeat or reenact great covenantal matters and to change the wording to fit the situation.

A commentary on the Ten Commandments would occupy more space than our specific goal permits so only the important factors about the Ten Commandments will be mentioned:

(1) They are not a list of general moral rules that are given by fiat to Israel. They are part of the covenant of the Lord with Israel and must be seen as covenantal terms as well as moral instruction. Such covenantal lists are well known to archaeologists.

(2) They have a redemptive basis. They are given by the God who redeemed Israel from Egypt. The first meaning of the Ten Commandments is that they are the morality of a redeemed people. Those who worship a holy God must also be holy. But it is also true that those who are *redeemed* by God are to be a moral people. And these commandments show that redeemed people are also people under ethical mandates.

(3) The Ten Commandments show that in biblical religion, religion and morality cannot be separated. The first four commandments are "religious" or "theological." The last six are ethical.

In the history of Israel and the church the Ten Commandments have actually been counted three different ways since they are not numbered in the text. Recent archaeological information would suggest that the first line considered by some to be a commandment is not a commandment but a typical introductory statement for a legal code. This could settle the way in which the Ten Commandments are to be numbered.

However coming back to the main point, right thinking about morality (the last six commandments) is based on a right understanding of God (the first four commandments). Philosophers may judge that ethics is possible without God or religion but this cannot be the case with the Ten Commandments.

(4) The commandments are very general. This is a blessing in the sense that being so general they are adaptable in so many cultures. This is also a burden because in the complications of life we do not know how to give particular interpretations to the commandments. For example, the commandment against murder is used to defend pacifism and to rebut capital punishment.

(5) The last six commandments represent the basic thesis of a community living together in peace. This becomes very apparent when the prohibitions are reversed and turned into positive affirmations.

Their possible function or usefulness to the church will be part of the discussion on law. All of them save the sabbath commandment appear as approved in the New Testament pages, and even the sabbath commandment is matched, at least partially, with the Christian first day of the week, or the Lord's Day.

(6) Their negative form is important as what is not forbidden is permitted. If they were positive assertions their character would be very restrictive and "negative" in a bad sense.

Section 102: The Sermon on the Mount

Chapters 5, 6, and 7 of Matthew contain the Sermon on the Mount, so-called because it takes place on an *oros* (mountain) in contrast to Luke's Gospel where it takes place on a *topos pedinos* (level place or plain).

It is customary for Matthew, especially from chapter 5 on, to arrange his material in topical groupings. The Sermon on the Mount represents one of these groupings and is therefore not to be understood as one speech given at one time but as a combination of elements from many speeches with the original core being what our Lord said on the mountain (cf. H. K. McArthur, *Understanding the Sermon on the Mount*).

(1) The speaker of the Sermon on the Mount is a unique teacher. It has been claimed that most of what our Lord said can be duplicated in rabbinical literature prior to his time. The uniqueness of the Sermon on the Mount is not that it is all new teaching, but is the manner and authority of the person who spoke it. Each line of it is validated by this person and the quality of his life as well as his unique authority. It is for this reason that the Sermon on the Mount stands with the Ten Commandments as one of the two greatest passages of ethical materials in Holy Scripture.

The uniqueness of the teacher is dramatically marked by the way he places his own authority higher than that of Moses and the rabbis with his "But I say unto you." It was this unusual boldness and unusual claim to authority which led the people to remark how his tone of authority was in contrast to the rabbis (Matt. 7:28). In rabbinic thought the greatest theologian of the Old Testament was Moses. It came as a real shocker for Jesus to put himself not only above the great rabbis of the past but above even Moses himself.

The only conceivable basis upon which he could do this was that he was the Messiah of Isaiah and the Son of Man of Daniel. He also claimed that the kingdom of God came with his coming, and in the letters of Paul he is the Lord of the church.

(2) The Sermon on the Mount was not a mere occasional speech in the history of ethics. It is surrounded by another entity and also embedded in it, and that is the kingdom of God (cf. Vernard Eller, *The Promise: Ethics in the Kingdom*). John the Baptist announced the coming of the kingdom; our Lord said that when he came the kingdom of God came nigh; and the kingdom itself is mentioned in Matthew 5:3, 10, 19, 20, 6:33, and 7:21. The Sermon on the Mount does not just hang in the air but might be called the ethical charter of the kingdom. It is part of the ongoing revelation and redemption of God as well as part of the kingdom of God and therefore must never be conceived as a self-contained ethical tract.

41

A great deal has been written in recent years on the concept of the kingdom, but it certainly represents the new rule of God, a rule that not only includes the cross and the resurrection of Christ but also the ethical considerations of the Sermon on the Mount (cf. George Ladd, *Jesus and the Kingdom*).

(3) The Sermon on the Mount shows that man as a moral person is going somewhere; he has a destiny. Its content is not single moral acts, but acts within the context of the kingdom, and the kingdom is *here,* it is *progressing,* and in some unique way it is *yet to come.*

The Sermon on the Mount contains such promises as entering the kingdom or inheriting the earth as well as very serious threats of judgment (Matt. 5:22, 29, 30).

The ethical content of the Sermon on the Mount is thereby tied in with the entire historical process of man, for it is part of the theology of the kingdom of God which in some senses is present but is also, *emphatically,* yet to come. In fact the very ending of the Sermon on the Mount in Matthew 7 indicates the kinds of destinies men may expect at the end of history. *It is an ethic which cannot be divorced from the eschatological aspect of the kingdom.*

From this perspective Christian ethics is misrepresented if it were *only* doing the right thing, *only* doing one's duty, *only* acting out of love and justice. These elements are not denied; what is denied is that they have sense or meaning outside of the theology of the kingdom of God.

(4) The Sermon on the Mount specifies that it is not a heretical innovation if heresy means that the moral importance of the Old Testament is denied. Jesus does not intend to lessen nor relax the ethical demands of the Old Testament (Matt. 5:19). What he did do was to introduce the concept of *fulfillment,* as seen in Matthew 5:17. In the ethical or moral aspect of the relationship of the two Testaments fulfillment means enlargement. The Old Testament ethic is partial or incomplete; the Sermon on the Mount fills it full with its real meaning. As far as the law went it served a limited and realistic service. Israel as an ancient culture could grasp and obey only so much. Now Israel and the human race is prepared for a larger, fuller, expanded meaning of the law. Hence the demands of the Sermon on the Mount are higher than the Ten Commandments.

(5) The Sermon on the Mount shows that additional dimensions must be added to moral behavior. Keeping the "letter" of the law is

not enough, nor is "external" conformity to law sufficient. The inward motivation must be as right as the external deed. To have an inward motivation that conflicts with the act done is hypocrisy. Right acts must grow out of the proper motivation, and wrong inward feelings can be sin as much as overt transgressions. In modern terms it could be said that morality is the *quality and harmony of life and action*. The moral man acceptable to God is the man whose motivation is proper and whose external act is right. How we think, how we feel, how we evaluate *internally* is as important to ethics as is conforming to proper ethical norms.

Section 103: The Golden Rule

The following verses contain the Golden Rule: "So whatever you wish that men would do to you, do so to them; for this is the law and the prophets" (Matt. 7:12 RSV). "And as you wish that men would do to you, do so to them" (Luke 6:31 RSV).

The first time the expression "Golden Rule" occurs is in 1674 when it was first called the "Golden Law," and then later the "Golden Rule." It was called "golden" because it was considered to be the supreme ethical maxim. It was called a "rule" to indicate its universal validity. It expresses the law of love which governs all Christian morality.

In the early Christian church this text created problems. To prevent abuse, phrases were added to it like "what good things" so that not *any* deed could qualify as fulfilling the meaning of the verse. However in the twentieth century the Golden Rule is taken as another maxim within the whole context of biblical ethics. There is more to ethics than the Golden Rule, and we know too much today about distorted human personalities to take the rule without necessary qualifications.

Its supreme worth is that it indicates the kind of attitude or spirit or policy of love and unselfishness that a Christian should have for his neighbor. But it cannot stand without qualification or understanding within the total context of New Testament ethics.

A great deal of research has been done to show that in its negative form ("don't do") it is found in several of the religions of the world and pagan philosophies. This is no great point, as Christian revelation does not mean that revelation to be revelation *must be totally new.* It only shows that men may stumble upon the truth of divine revelation without a special revelation. We can also observe this in Paul's sermon in Acts 17.

Paul Tillich's impressive little book, *Love, Power, and Justice,* is relevant here. He explains in this book how he relates these three terms. He is very much concerned that these concepts are not misrepresented or misunderstood. For example, a person may think he is expressing love in his generosity but he is really confirming his neighbor in his sin. Or power is not to be thought of like a force in the material world. Nor is justice something that is added to love, but justice is one of the ways love expresses itself. In like manner the Golden Rule no more stands alone than, as Tillich points out, any other ethical virtue does, for rules stand in interrelationships with other rules or moral principles.

Section 104: Love

The first suggestion of the primacy of love in biblical ethics is found in Leviticus 19:18 rsv: "You shall not take vengeance or bear any grudge against the sons of your own people, but you shall love your neighbor as yourself: I am the Lord." Jesus said that the whole of Old Testament morality rested (literally, "hung from") upon the love for God and the love for neighbor. Paul said that the love of one's neighbor was the fulfillment of the law (Gal. 5:14) and in the famous "love chapter" (1 Cor. 13) love is set forth as the supreme Christian virtue.

Much has been made by distinguishing *philia* (love more in the sense of friendship), *agapē* (love as free, gracious expression), and *eros* (love either as personal or selfish, or as sexual). But in the survey of great numbers of Greek texts it has been found out that such distinctions are relative for in many instances the words are used as synonyms.

A famous study of love was written in this century by Anders Nygren, *Agape and Eros.* Nygren has given us the essence of his thinking in an article on *Agape and Eros* in *A Handbook of Christian Theology* (p. 96 ff.).

Eros (from Plato) is essentially turned inwards, towards the personal wants, and therefore intentionally or not it has an element of selfishness in it. *Agape* is love as the New Testament teaches. It is manifested in God's love for sinful man, in the self-sacrifice of Christ on the cross, and in the giving of the benefits of salvation. It is outgoing love, gracious love, and sacrifical love.

Nygren has been criticized on the basis that the distinctions he makes cannot be consistently applied, but nevertheless his work is still the greatest work on the subject of love in our century.

When applied to ethics love has the following characteristics:

(1) On the first level, love is a positive feeling tone. It may have many elements such as affection, pity, sympathy, concern, and empathy. Ordinarily then to love is to *feel* a certain positive way towards another person. But this positive feeling of affection is not a necessary ingredient in every act of love in an ethical decision.

(2) Love is a policy to seek the good for others. The "good" has a thousand variations. It may be financial help; it may mean helping in a time of sickness; it may mean running an errand; it may mean interceding in behalf of; it may be an effort of mediation between divided parties; it may mean being considerate of a person that is despised by the rest of society. Love in ethics does not necessitate a certain feeling tone but it must be a policy of good—for a person, a group, a race, or a minority.

(3) Love as an ethical attitude is love that comes to concrete expression. The New Testament illustrates this: it is feeding the poor, clothing the naked, giving water to the thirsty, giving food to the hungry, looking out for the welfare of widows and orphans, and visiting the prisoners.

The greatest expression of love is that a man die for his friend, for that is by very definition the last and supreme act anybody can do out of love (John 15:13).

(4) Love is full of grace. Grace is love for the unlovely, love for the unworthy, and love for those who do not have the capacity to return love or even express gratitude. Real love makes no bargains and attaches no strings. Again in the New Testament we find how love expresses itself in grace. Our Lord talked, walked, and ate with the people on the bottom of the social scale in ancient Palestine—tax collectors, prostitutes, and lepers. There are many other ways in which our Lord demonstrated his love besides these more dramatic ones, but it is always unqualified love.

(5) Love is universal. Human love has a high degree of selectivity to it. Human love tends to restrict itself to *my* family, *my* relatives, *my* neighbors, *my* fellow workers, *my* social equals, and *my* ethnic or racial group.

Christian love may not be so parceled out. As such it is inconsistent. Love as an ethical norm crosses through all the barriers men make, jumps over the hedges they build, and ignores the insults of a people who resent the universal expressions of love.

To complete the analysis of the ethic of love in the New Testament would require at this point an exposition of 1 Corinthians 13. Since this would require many pages we will forego this exposition. We do suggest that the reader study this passage carefully within the context of its meaning for Christian ethics.

There are four kinds of ethical policies that collide with the New Testament ethic of love:

(1) *Legalism.* To be a legalist is to treat law, duty, and principles regardless of persons and their circumstances. "Doing one's duty" or "keeping one's principles" is more important than the welfare of persons. Loyalty to law is more important than loyalty to redemption, and keeping the code of one's religious "in-group" is more ethically serious than acts of love, forgiveness, and help toward fellow sinners. Only when law is interpreted in this narrow legalistic sense is law opposed to love. We cannot equate all law with legalism as situation ethics does (cf. J. J. Stamm and M. E. Andrew, *The Ten Commandments in Recent Research*).

(2) *Formalism.* To be a formalist is to believe that the universe is governed by inflexible moral standards. If these standards are not kept then the race will drown in a deluge of anarchy or immorality. Thus the form of the right, the form of the proper, the letter of the form is more commanding than the predicament of the person. Love is very hesitant ever to put a formal principle of ethics over the demands of kindness, pity, love, and help for people.

(3) *Sentimentalism.* Sentimentalism is the confusion of uncritical kind feelings with love. Love at times is hard and must be hard. A slap in the face or a stern denial may be the form that love must take. But sentimentality is kindness without conscience, sympathy without realistic assessment, goodness without reckoning with the softening process of treating a person with only good and never with discipline. Love seeks the good and avoids the destructive, but never at the price

46

of becoming uncritical, unsifted, blind emotionalism and sentimentalism. Love does not destroy moral fiber; sentimentalism does.

(4) *Selfishness*. Selfishness is a moral disease in which the outgoing spirit of love is turned inward and becomes love for one's self. It has many faces. It may be *egotism* where the person makes his self-love the value center of his universe. Or it may be *narcissism* where a person gives inordinate attention to his physical appearance, as well as inordinate amounts of time and money to be sure his wardrobe best displays his body. *Worldliness* is the excessive concern for our pleasure at the expense of the welfare of our neighbor. It is the introversion of love that seeks its fulfillment in the external pleasures that this world (world used here in its poorest sense) offers for the gratification of self-love (cf. 1 John 2:15–17).

These forms of selfishness are not to be confused with *egoism*. *Egoism* is the natural, normal, and necessary regard each person must have for his health and well being. The neglect of a healthy egoism is one of the signs of the beginning of mental deterioration.

Section 105: Justice

Love and justice are considered the cardinal ethical virtues. Men like Fletcher and Tillich try to reduce justice to love, or define justice as love implemented. There are some problems with this. First, it tends to make the concept of love so general that it is in danger of losing its necessary particularity. Second, there is the possibility that the hard moral fiber necessary for a real concept of justice is lost as justice blends into love. There is, however, no question of the very close relationship betweeen love and justice.

In a very excellent book, *The Biblical Doctrine of Justice and Law* (by Heinz-Horst Schrey, Hans Hermann Walz, and W. A. Whitehouse), the authors state that the basis of justice in Scripture is God's righteousness. They have something very particular in mind in affirming this. Justice is capable of being given very prejudiced interpretations. After fifty years of communism the Western nations have found out that the Communist ideology works within a different concept of justice than that of the Western nations. The point is not which is right and which is wrong, but that a biblical grounding of justice in the righteousness of God prevents any wrong definition of justice.

47

When we think of justice a number of synonyms come to mind which help us get the "hang" of the idea: the right, equity, fairness, impartiality, order, law, ought, fair play, and square deal.

Justice implies for us two fundamental concepts: that of right, and that of freedom.

(1) Every adult person should be treated by his fellow-man with the cluster of rights that belong to each of the following areas: social relationships, news media, business, contracts, advertising, politics, and the law. He also has the right to life (Gen. 9:5–6) and the right to be treated in honor (James 2:9). He furthermore deserves all those rights that belong to him relative to his status in life: e.g., as a man or woman, child or adult, employee or employer, young or old, crippled or healthy, etc.

(2) Every person has a claim to justice in the form of freedoms. Freedoms are those special things that can be determined by their own inner necessity and not by external imposition. It is therefore an injustice to infringe on a freedom.

For example, *religion* as the truth of God should be established by its own special criteria and not by political decree. The right man and the right law in *politics* should be established by the free, rational assessment of the voter and not by force. The theories of *science* are established by the methodologies established by the scientists as governed by the subject matter under investigation and therefore cannot be approved or refuted by church or state. A man has a moral responsibility for the conduct of his life and therefore his *conscience* must be respected.

The Holy Scriptures are saturated with materials on justice. This is because justice is related to law. If law is broken away from justice then law becomes pure convention or else the instrument of oppression and tyranny. The Christian stance is not merely to reproduce the biblical injunctives about justice and law (where in some cases it can) but rather to grasp the intention or the spirit or the implication of the justice and law of Scripture in order to make it a practical guide for contemporary moral decisions.

Justice too has its distorted versions:

(1) Injustice is forcing a theory or a policy, etc., upon a person or a group when such a theory or policy can be determined only in freedom and truth.

(2) Favoritism in all its forms (for example, nepotism) is to grant

rights, favors, or privileges to persons or groups on purely selfish and personal grounds without regard to worth, ability, qualification, or training.

(3) Brutality, persecution, and torture represent ways in which human dignity is treated unjustly or ways in which the punishment is in far excess of the crime. One of the most unfortunate chapters in human history is the belief that the devil or demons keep people from speaking the truth and only as they are tortured can they be released from the demons to speak the truth.

Section 106: Law in Scripture

This section is not concerned with law in the juridical sense but law as it appears in Scripture sometimes called the "Mosaic Law." Both the Hebrew word (*torah*) and Greek (*nomos*) have much wider meanings than this section intends. The key question is this: *what do the moral legislative elements of the Old Testament in particular have to do with Christian ethics?* Much of the New Testament is devoted to this theme (the Sermon on the Mount, Matt. 5–7; Rom.; Gal.; Phil. 3; and Heb.). Perhaps the most serious accusation the Jews could make against the church was that it was apostasy against Moses, the great law-giver (cf. Acts 6:11, 14; 21:21).

What then is the relationship of gospel to law?

(1) *Dispensationalism.* The dispensationalists believe that the law was given to Israel and Israel alone. It applies directly only to Israel and its function was to show man's failure before God under the law. The law was just, holy, and good but sinful man could not keep it.

The dispensationalists do not cut the law passages out of their Bibles. In that all of Scripture may be of profit to the Christian, the Christian may read the law with profit. The Sermon on the Mount is "pure law" yet "it has a beautiful moral application to the Christian" (*The Scofield Reference Bible,* second edition, p. 1000, fn. 2 from preceding page).

However to a dedicated dispensationalist one of the most serious errors a Christian can make in using Scripture is to mix law and grace, commandment and gospel. Although the Christian is not under the law he is not a moral anarchist as he is under the authority of the New Testament and under the guidance of Christ and the Spirit.

49

(2) *The Reformed View.* In the Reformed view man is always covenantly related to God. After man's fall from the Covenant of Works he is under a series of covenants of grace. The Mosaic Covenant (Exod. 12–14) is modified in that the dietetic and ceremonial aspects are null and void but the moral law is not. Such books as Galatians, Romans, and Hebrews enable the Reformed theologian to determine what is abolished in the Old Covenant with the coming of Christ and what is retained. The assumption seems to be that all those things not declared dated by the New Testament remain in force.

But this is no easy matter. Calvin was sensitive to the issues and wrote two chapters on it (*The Institutes of the Christian Religion,* Book II, Chapter X, "The Similarity of the Old and New Testaments," and XI, "The Difference Between the Covenants"). In modern times Barth goes a good measure beyond Calvin and says there is really only one covenant of salvation in the entire Scriptures and all the diverse covenants are different aspects of one covenant. The Mosaic Covenant represents the moral seriousness of the gospel.

Although in many doctrines the dispensationalists and the Reformed theologians agree, they do disagree violently on their interpretation of the law. The dispensationalists believe that the "covenant theologians" mix dispensations and so confound the unity or harmony of Scripture. They point out all the absurd things the Puritans did in trying to keep the law within the gospel. The covenant or Reformed theologians believe that the dispensationalists fracture the Scripture into seven dispensations and nine covenants (at least according to some dispensationalists), and make such a distinction between Israel and the church that shall remain through all eternity.

(3) *The Baptist Historic View.* The word "historic" had to be added because in America so many Baptists are also dispensationalists. Historically the Baptists have said that the New Testament is their rule of faith. This was never meant to disqualify the Old Testament or to be some kind of a new version of Marcion (a heretic of the second Christian century who divorced the New Testament from the Old). This assertion was made to counter all the Roman Catholic theology substantiated by allegorical interpretations of the Old Testament, and for Protestant theologians who were defending too much Christian ethics by recourse to the Old Testament.

Baptists insist that the church should build its theology and ethics from the New Testament. They reject the procedure which develops its ethic from the Old Testament, prunes off the ritualistic and cultic elements, and then adds the New Testament materials. To the contrary Christian ethics is to start with the New Testament and anything used in the church from the Old Testament must first be assessed in the light of the New Testament.

(4) *The Lutheran View.* The Lutherans' view of law and gospel is one of their most important doctrines and one of the hardest to get into focus. Lutheran theologians themselves have variant views of law and gospel which increases the problem for the non-Lutheran in grasping the doctrine. Complicating it even more are the four hundred years of controversy between Lutheran and Reformed theologians over the meaning of law and gospel. Barth's little booklet, *Gospel and Law,* didn't settle much and only opened old wounds especially when he reversed the Lutheran order of the terms. The problem is even more complicated when added to the law-gospel concept is Luther's concept of the two kingdoms. But some headway can be made.

First, this is not a division of the Old and New Testaments. There is law in the New Testament and gospel in the Old. Nor do the Lutheran theologians like the parallel expression of law and grace.

The Lutherans agree on two uses of the law and have a debate over the third:

Usus elenchticus. In logic, *elenchticus* means an argument which refutes another argument. The law is the case against the sinner. It is God's highest demand which no flesh can meet. It is then a word of judgment and wrath and therefore God's strange word. In preaching its function is to convict men of their sin and sinnerhood. It is to drive them to the despair that sends them to the cross.

The gospel is God's word of grace, love, and salvation in contrast to the law. It is God's offer of mercy and love in the person and sufferings of Christ. It is the good news of God, the proper action of God's saving right arm, and the sweet voice of God. Preaching of the law to produce despair is to be followed by preaching of the gospel whose purpose is to produce hope, then faith, and then salvation.

Usus politicus. Man as sinner needs to be restrained or controlled or regulated. This is the political use of the law and is intended for magistrates. Man as sinner cannot be controlled by gospel. Luther had a very realistic view of the devil. In the gospel Satan is combatted by redemption. The church fights the devil in society by the political use of the law.

51

Usus didactus or praecipuus. There is a debate among Lutheran theologians if there is a third use of the law wherein the law is a guide or help for the Christian (expressed by the phrase, *usus triplex legis*— three uses of the law). Even though the Christian is not formally under the law, the law does give him cues or ideas about what is righteous and holy and what is sinful or evil. In his booklet, *Law and Gospel,* Werner Elert, a leading Lutheran theologian of the twentieth century, sums up the issues. Elert believes that Luther taught only two uses of the law. The law does not have this "teaching" or "instructional" purpose for Christians.

Section 107: Summum Bonum—The Highest Good

The concept that there is a good greater than all goods or that there is a good which is the essence of all goods has a long history in Greek philosophy. It reached its greatest expression in Plato's philosophy in his concept of the good. Some interpreters equate it with Plato's idea of God.

In the Middle Ages the *summum bonum* stood for man's highest good, the vision of God. But since then in ethical theory it has become more a handy term to indicate what the final or supreme good is in a philosopher's ethics. Whatever is the best or the highest or the noblest in a moral philosophy is its *summum bonum.* Hence if a philosopher thinks that the essence of ethics is duty, doing one's duty is the *summum bonum.* If love is the supreme Christian virtue then love is the Christian's *summum bonum.*

Section 108: Duty

The word "duty" is derived from "due" and means then what one ought to do. In the broad sense that there is the right thing to do in contrast to a state of pure moral anarchy or relativism, *all* ethical theories are theories of duty. In a narrower sense an ethic of duty, or a *deontological ethic,* believes that man is under moral obligations, oughts, imperatives, demands, or commandments and ethics is "doing one's duties" or performing one's oughts. Duty in its strictest sense is absolute obligation and unconditional, and would have as its opposite such ethical theories as utilitarianism, hedonism, or situation ethics. Furthermore it is generally argued that what one's duty is, is just given; it is intuited; it is supplied by the conscience. In this latter sense the ethics of Butler is a duty ethics.

In the Christian tradition the Ten Commandments functioned as an ethics of duty. They were God's laws and as such were unconditional and universal and obligatory on all moral agents. Ethicists frequently claim that this creates a moralism or a legalism or a Victorianism or a Puritanism.

However, the chief defender of an ethics of duty was Kant. To him duty was a universal law. Order in society and integrity in people could be had only in an ethic of universal duty.

Kant has been given a narrow and a broader interpretation. The narrow interpretation is that he taught duty for the sake of duty. If a duty is a duty it is a *given*. One can't get behind a duty to show that it is a duty. Hence Kant's ethics has been considered loveless and impersonal. The broader interpretation is that Kant felt that ethics had to have the character of a moral imperative if ethics is to have any force or substance. Kant was not blind to persons, situations, and love but felt that these should not undermine the absolute serious character of ethical behavior.

Kant taken in his narrowest sense of duty for the sake of duty, as a universal obligation without qualification, has been strongly attacked in teleological ethics and in recent situation ethics. Perhaps one reason that Kant is given such a strict interpretation as a defender of a loveless ethics of duty is that he wrote a strong little article defending the thesis that it is never right to lie. The objectors to Kant suggest some situations in which telling the truth can create great evil, but Kant replies by showing that just the reverse could happen. The lie can backfire and create a greater tragedy than supposedly telling the truth would (I. Kant, *On a Supposed Right to Tell Lies from Benevolent Motives*).

Section 109: Casuistry

"Casuistry" comes from the Latin "casus" which means a case. Various ethical theories list rules, or principles, or standards, or oughts and the ethical person is the one who lives up to such standards.

But many times a person is confronted with a decision where the situation is confusing or complex or where rules conflict. Moral situations seldom come in neat little packages of either/or. Casuistry is the attempt to figure out what is the right action in a specific case when the case is complicated or the lines are blurred and the issues seem to conflict. The most recent attempt to deal creatively with this problem is that of E. L. Long, Jr., in *Conscience and Compromise: An Approach to Protestant Casuistry.*

Long makes it clear that compromise and casuistry can be the subject of abuse and exploitation and in this sense they are wrong. He is striving for a positive approach to the subject. Pascal's famous *Provincial Letters* exposed the manner in which the Jesuits abused the principle of casuistry. Long, on the other hand, wishes to construct a proper and morally defensible use of casuistry.

To explore all the problems involved in casuistry is to exhaust the subject of ethics itself. In fact one philosopher has said that ethics does not exist, only casuistry. There is one maxim on which treatises on casuistry agree: *casuistry should never be exploited so as to give an ethical justification of what is basically an unethical or immoral or deceitful action.*

Or stated positively it could be said: *casuistry can be practiced only when the moral agent is a person of moral integrity.*

Casuistry and compromise are inevitable. No person can avoid situations that spill over lines or that defy easy analysis. What does a man of moral integrity do when he must vote for one of two candidates both of which are bad characters? Does a parent treat a child severely for some act and unwittingly psychologically harm the child or treat the child in kindness and rob him of moral fiber? Debates about when to lie or be evasive or ambiguous or tell half the truth or the whole truth rage on and on!

When is a duty a cruelty and when is an exception a blunder? This is the cross every person of moral concern must carry. When must a decision be for an individual's betterment or for the betterment of society? Here is a game that must be played, but the rule book is confusing.

We have already stated two principles:

(1) Casuistry should never be exploited.

(2) Casuistry must always be undergirded by a person of moral integrity. And we add a third:

(3) The moral agent in a given situation must weigh the merits of the case, and he must bring to bear on the case all the relevant factors he can. Out of these three considerations the best possible decision can be made in a given case. Joseph Fletcher calls situation ethics "neocasuistry" to emphasize the uniqueness of each ethical situation.

Section 110: Ethics by Code

As indicated in the discussion of casuistry ethical situations are radically complex. One way of simplifying decisions is for a Christian community to accept a code, that is, a list of dos and don'ts and thus relieve the individual of making so many difficult decisions.

The Roman Catholic church, the Anglican church, and the Eastern Orthodox church have *canon law*. Canon law is not a list of ethical principles but more generally guidelines for the orderly conduct of church affairs. But some ethical elements are in canon law and so function as a code for that church. Groups known for having official or semiofficial codes are particularly the Pietists and the fundamentalists. However it must not be overlooked that most Christian groups do have a code written or unwritten. In fact some of the severest critics of "code morality" are themselves victims of such a tight code that they are utterly unaware of it. It is a psychological impossibility for any Christian group to exist without an open or hidden agenda of a code morality.

Although it is customary to be very critical of those groups who very openly guide themselves by codes, there are certain virtues in having a code:

(1) Adopting a code indicates a serious moral concern, however odd the code may be. Such groups of Christians consider purity, sanctity, and separation from that which corrupts an important element of Christian experience. They feel a laxity in these matters represents a decay from the standard of holiness found in the New Testament.

(2) Adopting a code gives a fellowship of Christians a cohesiveness. Any group, large or small, to hold together must have some kind of ideological inner core. A code of ethical dos and don'ts functions as a cohesive power to form a group into a unit and give a common spirit. There are certain virtues of unity, loyalty, understanding, and

mutuality that follow when a group of Christians agree to live according to a certain set moral pattern.

(3) There is an attempt in a code-ethic to be relevant. Evils not mentioned in Scripture need a Christian interpretation. The formation of a code helps Christians go from the generalities of Scripture to the particularities of life. As often as on the surface the code looks misguided, it is really an effort to be relevant.

The failings of a code-ethic are many and every group of Christians that emphasize a code-ethic must be aware of them: keeping the code creates the impression that one is keeping the whole counsel of God which is not the case; keeping codes is difficult when culture shifts and makes codes obsolete; code-ethics usually creates ingroups which interrupt the unity of the Spirit; and finally code-ethics is always guilty of swallowing camels and straining at gnats.

One of the reactions to code-ethics was the *adiaphora controversy.* *Adiaphora* is the Greek word for indifference. Pietism was a movement introduced into the Lutheran church with strong Calvinistic elements in it about so-called worldly amusements (dances, cards, etc.). Luther was a very earthy person and felt that all of God's good gifts were to be enjoyed, but Calvinism had an asceticism built into it. When this Calvinistic asceticism was introduced into the Lutheran church through Pietism, it set off a controversy. The strict Pietists wanted all worldly amusements banned for Christians. The traditional Lutherans thought that in these matters it was a case of personal choice. There was no real moral issue, hence, *adiaphora*—morally indifferent. The Christian man was a free man able to enjoy Christian liberty in the right sense—"Let every one be fully convinced in his own mind" (Rom. 14:5).

The fundamental issues about the *adiaphora* controversy are not limited to Lutheran churches. There have been, are, and always will be Christians who will to live by a code-ethic and brand certain activities as sinful amusements or at least amusements that weaken one's moral fiber. And there are Christians who feel that they are bound to what the New Testament teaches but beyond that there should be tolerance of practice and responsible Christian liberty. Part of this must certainly be psychological. People with very strict ideas of morality, or right and wrong, of spirituality and worldliness will defend a code-ethic and look at the *adiaphora* as slack Christian morality. Others who have a more tolerant, more open attitude towards life, less driven by conscience and moralism will want the least of moral restrictions and will let each Christian in Christian liberty decide what is proper for him and what is not.

Section 111: Asceticism

In Christian ethics there is the attempt to state that some things are wrong and some are right. We have also mentioned the hindrance of our sinful natures and the momentum gained by right motivation. But there is also another factor in Christian experience that has an extensive and complicated history, and that is asceticism. The original Greek word, *askeō*, meant to practice, to train, to exercise, to tame, to restrain. Asceticism in Christianity represents a great variety of schools of opinion. All such schools have one thing in common, namely, some sort of scheme or regime or practices that will enable the Christian to restrain sin, restrain temptation, restrain the body, and tame the passions so that the road to rectitude, morality, and sainthood may be achieved.

Asceticism is not peculiarly a Christian practice but may be found in most of the non-Christian religions.

Typical ascetic acts are:

(1) *Fasting*. Those who fast claim that once the hunger pangs let up the faster enters into a state of spiritual exaltation which enables him to attain levels of communion he cannot attain without fasting.

(2) *Celibacy*. Sexuality has played a complex role in religion (B. Z. Goldberg, *The Sacred Fire: The Story of Sex in Religion*). In some cultures sexual intercourse is actually part of the positive function of religion. For example, the famous Russian monk Rasputin belonged to the cult of Khlysty which had a ceremony lasting about three hours ending in sexual intercourse by the participants.

In other theologies it is believed that there is something inherently sinful or weakening in sexual intercourse so celibacy was one of the requirements for the soul to reach higher levels of spirituality.

(3) *Privation*. Some monks lived a life of absolute simplicity and hardship. They slept in caves, shacks, or dens, sometimes on doors or stone slabs and even without covers. Their diet was as simple as survival would permit. Hence the body was bruised into submission.

(4) *Isolation*. The founder of this order of monks was St. Antony

57

of Egypt (A.D. 251-356). At first these monks lived alone but later formed communities, but communities in isolation from the world.

(5) *Flagellation.* This was any type of physical punishment of the body. Some of it was mild and some of it was brutal. The theory was that the more the body suffered the freer the soul became for experience with God.

(6) *Renunciation and abstention.* A number of practices of the ordinary Christian were considered evil or weakening by the monks. Hence in many ways they pulled back or away from society. The Roman theater, the Roman arena, and the Roman games were all outlawed. If one were to compose a list of renunciations and abstentions made in the name of holiness in the history of Christian asceticism, it would make a book.

(7) *Taming or moderation.* This was a deliberate program to restrain the appetites, or to limit them, so that the normal appetites of the body would not weaken the aspirations of the soul.

The Reformers abolished a lot of the ascetic practices of the Roman Catholic church but there nevertheless grew up a number of ascetic groups within Protestantism—Pietists, Puritans, Fundamentalists, Holiness movements, Victorious Life or Overcoming movements.

There is asceticism in Holy Scripture. 1 John 2:15–18 warns of the corrupting power of the world. James 1:27 says the Christian ought to keep himself unstained from the world. Some of the prophets of the Old Testament lived ascetic lives. John the Baptist was ascetic in his life. Our Lord himself fasted and prayed. In 1 Corinthians 7:32–35 Paul argues for a very vigorous ascetic life. Perhaps his clearest ascetic pronouncement is 1 Corinthians 9:24–27 RSV: "Do you not know that in a race all the runners compete, but only one receives the prize? So run that you may obtain it. Every athlete exercises self-control in all things. They do it to receive a perishable wreath, but we an imperishable. Well, I do not run aimlessly, I do not box as one beating the air; but I pommel my body and subdue it, lest after preaching to others I myself should be disqualified."

The problem of asceticism is to differentiate what is pure privation devoid of any spiritual merit, and that which genuinely aids one's spirituality. The definitive passage that makes this differentiation is Colossians 2:16–3:4.

False asceticism, in this passage, is concerned with regulations about food, drink, festivals, new moons, sabbaths, worship of angels, ascetic debasement, and submission to purely human regulations. Paul objects to it because on the surface it promises so much but in reality it delivers nothing.

Asceticism has as its goal true spirituality. Paul says that the reality or substance that asceticism is talking about is really Christ (Col. 2:17); that true spiritual nourishment and power comes from fellowship with Christ, the Head, and not by empty ascetic practices (Col. 2:19); and that real spirituality is to be totally occupied with Christ who is our life (Col. 3:1–4).

In conclusion it may be said that:

(1) There is a true asceticism in Scripture as practiced in the Old and New Testament by great spiritual personalities.

(2) Asceticism is subject to abuse both theoretical and practical. Theoretically it can consider matter evil or sexuality evil even though these things are not in themselves evil. Practically it can be abused by heaping on Christians endless regulations that have no real spiritual power.

(3) There is no systematized asceticism in Scripture nor mandatory asceticism at least as an entire system. Christian liberty and Christian charity must prevail as each Christian seeks his best way to spirituality and the fulfillment of the Christian ethic. This seems in agreement with the spirit and principles set forth by Paul in Romans 14.

Section 112: Situation Ethics

In that situation ethics recognizes the primacy of love in Christian ethics, perhaps it should have been discussed in that section. But because it has become such a controversial matter it requires a special treatment. Our basic concern will be with Fletcher's opinions. Barth was a situation ethicist many long years ago. This comes out clearly in his decisions about the relative evils of nazism and communism. The former he vigorously condemned; the latter he did not. He justified his action on the basis that he is not guided by eternal principles but by concrete situations. Therefore his response to the Communists was different from his response to nazism because two different situations existed between them. He claims, therefore, that he cannot be declared inconsistent in criticizing Hitler, and not criticizing communism (Karl Barth, *Against the Stream*). Since all this is buried in his huge tomes and lost to the American public who were not in the position to be sensitive to how Barth felt and reacted to the situation, he made no great ethical impact upon America. But he was a situation ethicist before Fletcher. Bishop Robinson's book, *Honest to God,* defends a situation ethic in his chapter on "The New Morality." And there is a situation element in Bonhoeffer when he speaks of there being ethical situations more than ethical principles, and that ethics can never be discussed abstractly but only concretely as instances of "the formation of Christ" (Dietrich Bonhoeffer, *Ethics*). Thomas C. Oden's *Radical Obedience: The Ethics of Rudolph Bultmann* shows that the essence of Bultmann's ethics is essentially a situation ethics.

The basic materials are: Joseph Fletcher, "Six Propositions: The New Look in Christian Ethics," printed in *The Harvard Divinity Bulletin,* October, 1959; and his two books, *Situation Ethics* and *Moral Responsibility: Situation Ethics at Work.* Then there are two compilations containing the controversial articles and reviews of Fletcher's position: *Storm over Ethics* and *The Situation Ethics Debate.* For the person who is really interested in all the phases of this debate there is no other alternative than to read this basic literature. We intend only to give some perspectives on the issue:

(1) In reading Cox's introduction to the book he edited (*The Situation Ethics Debate*) one readily learns that "Joe Fletcher" is an unusual personality. Therefore much is lost by getting only a bookish impression of this man. One has to read his writings not only as so much ethical theory and ethical cases, but as the product of a very unusual and remarkable personality—an understanding that would enable us to get some of his opinions in better focus.

(2) There are really two Fletchers. When he wants to bounce somebody out of a rut, he makes very shocking statements or extremely unconventional statements. When he does this he seems to to be talking not about an ethic of love but of anarchy. Yet the second Fletcher renounces *antinomianism* (which is unrestrained freedom), claims that we can't think ethics without *facts,* and demands that we know something about the *principles* or *rules* or *policies* in the history of Christian ethics. To be fair to Fletcher one has to quote *both* Fletchers.

(3) Fletcher knows that modern life is so complicated that it is impossible to follow neat or simple ethical rules or codes. He therefore employs shock treatment. He presents the reader with very unusual and complicated cases in which he can show that any traditional ethical

rule falls flat on its face. The Christian who thinks he has all the basic rules in the New Testament which he can readily apply (and must only occasionally worry about a complex case) is not living in the center of life in the twentieth century. Fletcher specializes in those agonizing kinds of situations where traditional ethical procedures are helpless or inadequate and if applied literally would be either cruel or nonsensical.

(4) Therefore he tries to restructure Christian ethics so that it can be relevant in our complex civilization. He does this by suggesting that there is only one moral imperative or absolute and that is love. And he partially agrees with Robinson in *Honest to God* that love confronted by a given moral situation knows how to "home in" on the right act. We may have some general ideas ahead of time but when it comes to the specific act we must first know the specific situation and then ask "how does love find its way through this situation?" In this way Christian ethics can be realistically practiced in our century.

(5) Certainly part of Fletcher's popularity is that he has caught the mood of the hour. He speaks to situations which people by the thousands encounter every day. In a time when people are restless with moralisms, when older ethical principles fail for real justification, when human freedom is being pushed even further than before, Fletcher's situation ethics seems to have the same beat. If one were to read a book on moral theology written about 1920 and then read Fletcher, it wouldn't take too much reflection to understand why the 1920 book would seem sterile, dated, and unrealistic, and why Fletcher seems to be "right with it."

With two whole books and endless magazine articles concerning Fletcher, it is difficult to reproduce all the objections to his position. Certainly not all of them are valid. Our attempt here will be to show only the *kinds* of objections that are made against him (which must be seen in terms of the qualifications of his system presented in the previous paragraphs):

(1) *Situation ethics is too individualistic.* This objection takes many turns. If each person in each situation must make up his own mind then any such concept of universal principle, eternal moral truth, or abiding ethical norms is shot down. And ethics cannot be taught as just a series of disconnected, disjunctive statements or decisions.

Or, Fletcher is an existentialist. He pulls down walls; he erases lines; he destroys sanctions; he makes ethical decisions solitary existential leaps. In fairness to Fletcher it must be stated that he denies that his ethics is unrelievable existentialism.

His ethics fractures the Christian community, for instead of the church moving through history with a common moral heritage, each Christian is reduced to an ethical island of his own, making his decisions on the basis of love as he as a person, and not the church as the body of Christ, understands love.

If ethical situations are as *unique* as Fletcher makes them out to be then nobody knows what to do in a given situation, not even Fletcher. Intelligent decision making is based on experience, precedent, and analogy. But if the ethical situation is *unique* all these criteria fail and love does not know how to *home in* on the right decision.

(2) *He ignores the seriousness of sin.* Love may be the supreme rule. But love is always exercised by sinners and sinners can be very confused about what love truly is. Therefore something must be added to love so that sinners can have some idea how love does concretely express itself. To leave a man with love and love alone to guide him ethically is not so much antinomianism (which Fletcher rejects) but it is unabashed Pelagianism. (Pelagius was a British monk who came to Rome about the year 400 A.D. He violently challenged the views of Augustine about sin and depravity. He defended the thesis that Adam did not bring the entire human race into a state of sin, nor do we inherit any sin or guilt from Adam. To the contrary man can save himself by his own efforts. The grace of God is not an indispensable necessity but merely an added help. In theological discourse *Pelagianism* has come to mean any optimistic view of man, any unrealistic assessment of sin and depravity, and any view of salvation or ethics which does not require supernatural grace or the necessary assistance of the Holy Spirit.)

(3) *He reverses the ordinary way in which a science is constructed.* Sciences work from their positive, normal results to theory. Odd factors are at the edge and constitute problems for future research. But to start with the atypical, the unusual, in the formation of a science is impossible. Thus Fletcher's use of the unusual case as the point of departure for his ethics is a kind of procedure that could never be followed in any other sciences. In fact if it were, it would wreck ordinary science for the unusual instance would throw all established results into the shadow of serious doubt.

Furthermore going from the extreme case to ethical theory confuses the layman. The kinds of unusual situations that Fletcher cites are not the daily things which confront Christians. The bulk of their ethical decisions are "right down the middle." To throw the weight of ethical theory on the unusual case leaves the ordinary Christian stranded with his routine ethical decisions.

(4) *He presumes his interpretation of the unusual situation is correct.* Fletcher cites a very difficult case. He then gives his interpretation. Then follows the presumption that his interpretation based on situation ethics is the correct one which resolves the problem, and that the older "legalistic" or "Puritanical" ethic is helpless to know what to do, or if it does suggest something it is very damaging. However the victory in argument is not to be had so easily or cheaply. There is still the possibility of a stiff and even convincing argument for the decision of the older ethic.

(5) *The New Testament does not divorce love from specifics.* Both Jesus and Paul taught that love was the supreme ethic (Matt. 22:38–39, Rom. 13:10, 1 Cor. 13). But both added many other ethical norms to their belief in the centrality of love. At least in Jesus' mind and in Paul's mind there was no contradiction in asserting the primacy of love and then adding to that whatever you wish to call them—norms, principles, rules, moralisms, legalisms.

This may be said another way. When love and love alone is the moral guide it becomes so general, so inflated, or so flexible that it either becomes useless or wretchedly difficult to apply. When *specifics* are given as Paul and Jesus gave them, we have some idea which direction love takes.

(6) *Moral principles need not be stated as narrow specifics.* Morality may be stated in terms of programs, policies, or attitudes, but not as inflexible rules. If this is the case then the charge against them that they are legalistic or Puritanical is baseless. Fletcher recites one case where "sacrificial adultery" resolves a very difficult situation. But his critics point out that the *one* act of "sacrificial adultery" could lead to a career of "sacrificial adultery" to resolve difficult problems. And nothing in Fletcher's assumptions could judge an entire career of "sacrificial adultery" as wrong.

(7) *Fletcher reduces all law to legalism.* But this is not true to much Scripture. The Hebrew word for law, *torah,* and the Greek, *nomos,* are much too wide in their meaning to be synonyms for legalism. Further, the elaborate praise of the law in Psalm 119 shows

that all law cannot be reduced to legalism. If all law cannot be reduced to legalism, then Fletcher's program is fractured.

It is popular today to damn a position in ethics by saying it is legalistic or Puritanical. Granted a number of cruel, stupid, and senseless things have been done by Christians in the past. Is modern ethical theory suddenly going to undergo a perfectionism or sanctification that will free it from its own cruelties, stupidities, and senseless advice? Have "legalism" and "Puritanism" really been given an honest and a fair hearing in our day? Have its critics taken into account cultural factors? Or to say it differently, have they not been unrealistic in asking more from former Christian ethics than can be expected from it in view of the cultural conditioning of every century? In our judgment there are a number of such uncriticized and unsifted presumptions in situation ethics.

Furthermore, have Christians in the past been purely moralistic in ethics? or purely legalistic? or purely Puritanical? Has there not been justice tempered with love in all generations? Can it be readily defended that all Christian people were heartless or unbending or disregarding of concrete situations in their ethical decisions?

In the history of Christian ethics there have been some sad chapters. Our contention is that in defense of situation ethics the ethical conduct of Christians of the past and the ethical theories of other generations have not been given a fair assessment. There *has* been regard for persons, regard for situations, and concern with the primacy of love in previous Christian generations. Past Christian conduct has not been all legalistic, moralistic, and Puritanical. There has been an element of the contextual or situational in Christian ethics in all periods even though it was not recognized as such. Fletcher's great service is to make us very much aware of what has been at the fringes. And he has attempted to give these elements some systematic formulation and illustrates how they can serve in specific situations. We can learn from him mistakes of the past, and some ways to be relevant for the present problems without a different formulation of basic ethical theory.

III

OBJECTIONS TO CHRISTIAN ETHICS

Section 200: Philosophical Tensions

Whenever theologians believed that there was some sort of natural affinity between Christian revelation and a specific philosophy, there has not been a significant tension historically between philosophical ethics and theological ethics. Thomas Aquinas would be a case in point.

However a great intellectual revolution took place in Europe a century after the Reformation. It had a different name and a different expression in each country. In England it was called deism; in France the leaders of such new thought were called "the philosophers"; in Germany they were called rationalists or materialists. The intellectual revolution in Germany called the Enlightenment was very influential in changing both the thinking of Europeans and their mind set. This revolution rejected orthodox Christianity and either drifted away from the church or became very skeptical about it.

In the territory of ethics there is propounded an *autonomous* ethics (ethics developed within the discipline of philosophy) and a *heteronomous* ethics (an ethic derived from the church or Holy Scripture or religion). It could not be otherwise than that a strong Christian theology with an articulate Christian ethics would collide with a philosophical system of ethics.

A theologian believes in the divine imperative; the philosopher works with a "categorical imperative" which has been derived from his philosophical analysis.

A theologian accepts the sovereignty of God as the ultimate source and authority of ethical norms; the philosopher works with the autonomy of man, namely, that man within his own powers can come to ethical principles sufficient for his own guidance.

A theologian believes that sin permeates all of man's actions and this includes how and what he thinks about ethics; the philosopher confines his remarks to general human weakness or the ready way man may be corrupted by evil forces in his society.

A theologian believes that divine revelation has been given not only for man's salvation but for the moral guidance of the redeemed man; philosophers confine themselves to intuitions or analyses or what may be gleaned from experience.

A theologian believes in a God who saves and redeems. By the very nature of the task of philosophy itself, philosophical ethics has no provision for a God of redemption nor the act of salvation.

A number of the essays in I. T. Ramsey, *Christian Ethics and Contemporary Philosophy,* challenge the thesis that ethics is dependent upon religion. A typical one is by Kai Nielsen, "Some Remarks on the Independence of Morality from Religion," (chap. 8).

This does not mean that Christian ethics ignores philosophical ethics. There is much to be learned from philosophical ethics as well as deriving from philosophical ethics some real correctives for Christian ethics. Theologians have not stopped reading secular ethics and they do not neglect philosophical ethics today. It is part of being competent in the field of ethics.

The truth of the matter is that there is a deep cleavage between Christian ethics and philosophical ethics at the point of autonomy or heteronomy. A theologian thoroughly dedicated to the reality of divine revelation, and a philosopher who will accept only an autonomous or philosophical ethic, will continue indefinitely in a state of contradiction, but we hope in mutual respect.

Section 201: Psychological Objections

In 1914 John Watson wrote his famous work, *Behavior: An Introduction to Comparative Psychology.* Either an external or internal sensory organ (or nerve ending) is stimulated which sends an impulse into the brain. The brain directs the impulse to glands or muscles where there is a response. This response is behavior and this is what psychologists study. There is no mind nor soul nor spirit nor conscience in a traditional sense. There is only stimulus and response-behavior. In such a system there is no right nor wrong, no true nor false, no holiness nor sin. All such categories are read into man's behavior by man. In such a psychological system ethics at best would consist of explaining why people label such actions as right or wrong. It would be a purely descriptive ethics.

The specific theory of Watson was wrecked by later experimentation. Today the expression "methodological behaviorism" is used. This means that psychologists cannot get inside the brain (or if you please, the mind) and therefore are confined to observing behavior. But this can be done without accepting the philosophical behaviorism of Watson. However most psychologists do not make moral judgments about human behavior. There is yet no soul, no spirit, and no moral monitor. Man's actions psychologically considered are amoral and the only kind of ethics possible is a descriptive ethics which would attempt to explain the psychological and sociological reasons people insist on calling behavior moral or immoral.

Other objections to a system of ethics come from the clinical psychologists. To them man is a "driven" creature. His actions may seem free but in reality they are not. Man is always under pressure either at the conscious or unconscious level. Forces in the unconscious can put enormous pressures on man's conscious acts. That which makes man function are habits, defense mechanisms, repressed experiences or suppressed memories. If a psychologist is Freudian or Jungian in his orientation he believes there is a vast and powerful territory below the level of consciousness, the unconscious, that greatly determines a man's behavior. If this is taken as the total picture of man, then such concepts as morality, conscience (except as superego), and ethical norms are but conventional fictions. Man is essentially amoral and again ethics is descriptive and not prescriptive. There are only healthy or adequate responses, or sick and inadequate ones; but none is intrinsically right or intrinsically wrong.

To sum up, a strict behavioral approach to man sees man's actions as amoral and ethical judgments are purely external interpretations of the actions of men. From the standpoint of clinical psychology or psychiatry man is driven by a number of psychological forces which are amoral and therefore ethical judgments are purely external interpretations.

There is another objection from psychologists. They affirm that very few people are really controlled by religious and/or ethical beliefs. For example, tests given to students on cheating or honesty show little correlation between what a student believes and what he does in a test situation. The student's goal is to pass that test and if cheating helps, he cheats regardless of his religious or ethical code. This reenforces the psychologist's conviction that behavior is essentially amoral and that ethical systems do not realistically function among people.

In reply to this a few brief remarks may be made:

(1) The Christian ethicist believes that the expression "man is a free moral agent" is a fiction. He also believes that the assertion that man is an amoral creature is a fiction. The ethical acts of men are imbedded in all that man does. Ethical convictions do not exist as abstractions or as items isolated from the total personality of man. The presence of other factors qualifies ethical decisions; it does not destroy the ethical in man.

(2) Ethical behavior is selective in the most moral man. A student who cheats on an examination may be very moral in most of the other aspects of his life. The very moral housewife may engage in some unethical tricks in her shopping. A student who may do a lot of stealing from his dormitory mates will endure any kind of academic punishment rather than "rat" on one of the very students from whom he has stolen. Being a moral person does not necessarily mean being consistently moral in all situations as if a moral person were immune to any sort of temptation or strong pressure from his peers or the "social necessity" of passing certain courses.

Furthermore psychologists who make tests on morality or ethics must be moral and ethical in their scientific methodology. Ethical rules are the very fiber of the scientific method and any psychologist who violated them would jeopardize his professional standing. Before a psychologist writes off all behavior as amoral he had better check on how the scientific method would work if it contained no standards about being ethical or honest.

Section 202: Friedrich Nietzsche (1844–1900)

As unconventional as Nietzsche was, as sick and neurotic as he was, he remains one of the great philosophers of the nineteenth century. He concerns us because his attack on Christian ethics was the most ruthless one in the history of ethics. In defense of Nietzsche it must be said that few men have ever lived whose entire intellectual energy and passion for truth was as great as Nietzsche's.

Nietzsche shared with some of the other philosophers of his century the view that the central or important part of man was not his reason nor that the world and history were essentially rational. Schopenhauer had the greatest effect on Nietzsche, for Schopenhauer taught that the universe was a blind, irrational striving and driving of Will. Later on Nietzsche gained some support for his theories from Darwin's idea of the survival of the fittest (i.e., of the superior).

Because Nietzsche had such nonrational views of man and the universe, he is frequently listed as one of the anticipators of existentialism. Nietzsche believed that the culture of the West was on its way out. A new order was coming, the order of the superman. The superman was going to remake ethics. This remaking of ethics is called "the transvaluation of all values." It is based on the distinction between slave morality and master morality. Christianity advocated a slave morality with its love, sentimentalistic attitudes, mercy, pity, etc. Master morality is the morality of superman which emphasizes courage, the mastery of the self, the possession of clear vision, and being the rugged, independent individualist.

Much modern social evil has been traced to Nietzsche. Some have thought his philosophy was at the bottom of World War I. The Nazis tried to use his writings for their propaganda but the attempt failed. He is even a hero to some thinkers today because he diagnosed so brilliantly the decadent culture of the nineteenth century and summoned man to a new mode of existence. However we assess the man— as a prophet, an existentialist, or as a critic of culture—he nevertheless stands as a man whose attack on Christian ethics was as brutal as possible, especially in *The Antichrist.*

Section 203: Emotive Theory of Ethics

In the nineteenth century a quiet but impressive revolution took place in the deeper understanding of logic, mathematics, and geometry. The advances in science such as the relativity theory and atomic physics were more popularly known. A group of philosophers, scholars, and scientists living in Vienna in the 1920s held a Thursday night discussion group to see what these changes meant for philosophy. Due to the international crises associated with Hitler and World War II most of these men fled to other parts of the world, particularly England and America.

The kind of philosophy these men advocated has had a number of names as the philosophy itself expanded from its original base. Originally it was called the Vienna Circle, then logical positivism, then logical empiricism, and later linguistic analysis. Today it is generally called analytic philosophy.

It of course has had many things to say about ethics and that is our particular concern. For the person who wants to be initiated into the ethical thinking of this school without being swamped by technicalities, we suggest Mary Warnock's book, *Ethics since 1900*. A. J. Ayer's little book, *Language, Truth and Logic,* was very influential in introducing these ideas in England and chapter 6, "Critique of Ethics and Theology," gives the essence of the objections of this school to ethics as traditionally understood.

From the inception of this new philosophy in the 1920s until the present it has undergone many changes including changes in ethical theory. Our immediate goal is to set forth how this school looked at ethics prior to some of the later modifications. Understanding the original position of this school will then be the basis for understanding the modifications which did come.

This school of thought specializes in what is called *linguistic analysis*. This means that it attempts to classify sentences. It makes a distinction between the *grammatical structure* of a sentence and its *logical character*. "Chairs exist" and "God exists" are grammatically identical in form. But in logical character they are very different. This becomes apparent when the question is asked: How do you know a chair exists, or, that God exists?

One whole class of sentences is called *formal*. This means they refer only to symbols. These sentences say nothing of the way the world is put together. Thus logic, mathematics, geometry, and rules of grammar are made up of *formal sentences*.

If a sentence proposes to say something about the world, it is a *material sentence*. Thus "it is raining today" is a material sentence since it describes a state of affairs in the world.

Our concern is with material sentences so we will ignore formal sentences.

In looking at material sentences we must first keep in mind that *grammatical* similarity and *logical* similarity are two different things. Sentences that are grammatically the same in structure may be very different in their logical character. This we have already illustrated by the two sentences, "chairs exist" and "God exists."

This calls for a second distinction. Material sentences are *meaningful* or *meaningless;* they make *sense* or they make *nonsense.*

If something can be empirically done about a sentence, the sentence is meaningful or it makes sense. "There are thirty students in the classroom" is a meaningful sentence because the students can be counted. I can do something empirical or factual or experimental about the sentence. The sentence thus makes sense. It has a logically empirical form.

If I say that "there are thirty green elves in the room," this sentence is meaningless or senseless. I cannot see green elves. I have no way of counting them or detecting them. The logical form of the sentence then is meaningless or senseless.

But this is different from a sentence being true or false. There might be only twenty students in the class. But I can count them. I can see them and number them. The claim that there are thirty may be false, but it is not *meaningless* in that I can do something about the sentence. A sentence may be meaningful or make sense because I can do something empirically about it, but it is actually false.

But to assert that there are green elves in the room is not false; it is meaningless. There is no conceivable empirical action that I can take that will detect these elves. The sentence is then *senseless* even though it is a grammatically correct sentence.

When such linguistic analysis is applied to art, religion, and ethics we discover that the kinds of sentences in these subject matters are meaningless or senseless. They are grammatically correct but from the standpoint of their logical character they are meaningless. According to this school, what can be done about such statements as: "the soul is simple," "the soul is immortal," "God is," "it is wrong to lie," "this picture is beautiful"? The answer is *nothing*. None of these sentences can be verified factually, or empirically, or experimentally. They are not false sentences but meaningless or nonsense sentences. Hence statements about ethical norms are meaningless or senseless.

Of course a psychologist may investigate why a person says "be honest," or a sociologist may study why a culture believes adultery is wrong and in this sense ethical statements have a meaning. But as statements expressing facts they are meaningless or senseless because from the examination of their logical character they do not express a fact.

An ethical statement, however, does say something. It registers how I feel about cheating or stealing or killing, etc. The Vienna Circle called their study about the feelings of people in so-called ethical situations the *emotive theory*. Others have called it the *exhortatory* theory of ethics. The logical form of an ethical statement is: "Would that all people would not cheat." Others have called it *policy ethics*. An ethical system is not true or false because its maxims cannot be verified or falsified. But they may indicate how I will act from day to day. It may also be called the *socially viable* theory. No philosopher can prove an ethics to be true or false. Ethics is the kind of material that cannot be treated this way. But since millions of people live on the same planet there must be some rules unless civilization degenerate to chaos. Ethical rules, then, serve as social controls enabling millions of people to live together. Hans Reichenbach of the analytic school writes in his book, *The Rise of Scientific Philosophy,* that in Rome do as the Romans do. Democracy is the way of life in America so be democratic. There is no logical or scientific or empirical force behind all this, for ethical sentences are meaningless or senseless. But there is social utility and so as long as we are on this earth living in a certain country, the way of prudence is to go with the acceptable ethical system simply for the ethical utility of such a policy.

There have been modifications of the emotive theory of ethics, but nonetheless the Christian gets the message in each of its versions. Christian ethics as offering norms, standards, rules, principles, or policies that are binding on men in that they are moral creatures before God is ruled out. The various versions of ethics developed in the linguistic tradition are at variance with the manner in which the Christian faith understands the nature of ethics.

It would be unfair to stop our comments at this point for there are Christians who think in the tradition of analytic philosophy. The shift from verificational analysis to functional analysis, and the idea of language games, has loosened up the old doctrinaire logical positivism. Now that it has been loosened up there are Christian theologians who believe that Christian ethics can be explained from the standpoint of analytic philosophy. Our point is that in its origin this philosophy was completely antagonistic to the Christian understanding of an ethical norm, and that those philosophers who follow the modern version of linguistic analysis are as much opposed to Christian ethics as the original Vienna Circle. The Christian version of linguistic ethics as worked out by such a philosopher as Jerry Gill is beyond our intention.

Section 204: Sartre

There are different versions of existentialism but the version most hostile to Christian ethics is that of Sartre. Sartre said he was going to devote an entire book to ethics which he never wrote. His ethical theory has to be gleaned from his writings. Different commentators on existentialism or interpreters of Sartre have tried to reconstruct his ethics (cf. M. Warnock, *Existentialist Ethics* or the chapter on ethics in Régis Jolivet, *Sartre: The Theology of the Absurd*).

Our concern is not to restate the ethics of Sartre but to indicate the places of major conflict with Christian ethics.

(1) *There is no such thing as a fixed or established human nature.* Man is freedom and man is condemned to freedom. In his freedom man makes himself. This does not mean an ethical anarchy to Sartre for two reasons: (i) each man has a vision, an intuition that other people are subjects like he is and not just other objects; (ii) therefore when a man acts in his freedom he is acting for all men. But man in the image or likeness of God is not possible with Sartre. There is no image of God in man which man in turn is to realize in his religious and ethical life.

(2) *There are no such things as innate moral ideas.* Man is not born with his mind laden with potential or actual moral standards.

(3) *There is no natural law.* Natural law, as we have seen, has been a common ground for Greeks, Romans, Roman Catholics, and Protestants. But if man is born to freedom and condemned to freedom, then there is no natural law.

(4) *There is no God.* At times Sartre does speak of God but only as a functional or limiting concept. But there is no God in the traditional Christian sense. If there were such a God then man would be obligated to obey his moral principles. To obey somebody else is to lose one's freedom even if that other one is God. There cannot be both God and freedom.

Sartre has a complicated doctrine of "bad faith" which is wider than his ethical theory but included in it. In simplest terms a person acts in bad faith when he acts according to some external consideration, something heteronomous. To make an ethical decision on the basis of force or coercion or demand—choose your verb!—is to be guilty of bad faith.

(5) *Authenticity is the only real standard of an ethical act.* When a man is faced with an ethical situation there is really no right or wrong choice as in traditional ethics. There is only authentic choice or bad faith. A choice is authentic when it is the expression of the genuine person or when it is the real actualization of his freedom.

During World War II there was a plot to assassinate Hitler by some of his own German people. To one man this would be murder. He could not act in freedom or authenticity to kill Hitler. But another person might feel that this is what is necessary for his freedom and authenticity. There is no right or wrong in killing Hitler. Not killing Hitler is right for one man, and killing Hitler is right for another, for the true measure of moral action is authenticity. It is not conforming to traditional ethical rules. To act on that basis is to be guilty of bad faith.

Not all Christian theologians are critical of Sartre. Christian theologians who think favorably towards existentialism and Sartre's demand for authenticity and real freedom in ethical decision believe that he is closer to a genuine Christian ethic than typical church morality which people conform to not out of genuine moral concern but to "fall into the pattern" and not offend other Christians. Such considerations may cause one to modify a harsh judgment of Sartre but it should not be pushed to the point where the real antiChristian elements in his ethical theory are overlooked.

Section 205: Civil Law

One of the more influential theories of law in the past fifty years is that the function of law is social control. Civilization, business, and industry can exist only within a set of laws, lawyers, courts, and judges. The law functions similar to an umpire or referee to keep the game honest. This may also be called a positivistic view of the law in that it sees its role as purely functional.

74

The tradition of law that started with Moses in Exodus and Leviticus looked upon law as the expression of the righteousness of God. In more modern terms the law was to be obeyed because it was the form that justice took in civil affairs. The law was kept and enforced on the basis that it represented the justice of God, and was not a convenient system of rules for business and government. Whatever law was enacted (apart from ordinances or conventional rules) was underwritten by the belief that it was an expression of justice.

The Christian does not doubt that law functions as social control. He also admits that many laws are purely conventional or expedient as typified in the endless ordinances of the legal system of any large city. But if law is purely conventional, purely for social control, functionally operating purely as umpire, then there is nothing binding or holy about law. Law is not the concrete expression of a universal concept of justice.

Into this situation came the Nazis, Fascists, and the Communists. Here law was interpreted as social control *with a vengeance*. The leader or the clique made the rules. There were rubber-stamped laws, unlawful arrests, rigged trials, and torture all in the name of social control. What could a jurist say against this system if he believed that law was *only* for social control, *only* an umpire, or only a *convention?* He actually had no theoretical basis for objecting to this practice. If he appealed to humanism or democracy this appeal had no more grounding than law as social control.

The only corrective to this is the return to the biblical notion that law is the concrete expression of justice, and where laws violate justice they are not laws. On this basis a jurist could speak a strong word of protest to the Nazi or Fascist or Communist interpretation of law.

This is a very general exposition and oversimplified. But it is intended to make a point—that law is the expression of justice and justice is the expression of the righteousness of God. And here and here alone is the real point of attack upon all systems of law that are theories of social control and used by tyrannies to suppress and persecute the common man.

Section 206: Ethics and the Absolute State

That private citizens or groups within a state have had differences with the policies of the state itself is no new thing. Nor can it be denied that in the history of the state since 5,000 B.C. there have been absolute states, i.e., states claiming final and absolute power or authority in all matters.

With the advent of reflective ethics and political philosophy by the Greeks, and the notion from Holy Scripture that states as well as individuals are subject to higher laws, the state could no longer be considered absolute. It was sometimes vaguely understood and at other times articulated that the state was to embody justice, and if it totally failed in this, revolution was justifiable.

However, in German idealistic philosophy of the nineteenth century the relationship of state to individual took a new turn. The essential unit of humanity was no longer the person or the citizen but the state. Therefore in all matters of conflict between state and individual the state was to have the right of way. This included ethics and morality. At this point in ethical and political thought the kind of thinking in which the state began to take on absolute power was still theoretical and bookish.

But the idea of a state as the final or ultimate unit of society and therefore an absolute state became fact not theory in the twentieth century. It is frequently called *statism*. The three common examples given of statism are Germany under Hitler, Russia under Stalin, and Italy under Mussolini.

The form statism took in each of these instances was different as was the justification. But certain theses were held in common. It was the state that *really* knew what was best for the common man. The idea of *individual conscience* was a decadent hangover from the past or the rationalization of selfishness. Part of the function of the state was to determine morality. *Thus legality and morality became identical.*

The state was under no higher jurisdiction or sanction than itself. It was omnicompetent and could legislate morality as well as other kinds of laws.

This is in direct contradiction to Christian ethics. Both man and state are under higher mandate, and that mandate is the justice or righteousness of God. For example in the early days of the Communist revolution in Russia it was stated very plainly that murder, brutality, etc., expressed against the state were wrong; but if murder, brutality, torture, or persecution fostered the progress of the state it was moral.

There is no question that one of the most difficult problems facing Christians is in states which put state morality over individual conscience, and make criticism of the state a crime.

Section 207: The Four Options

There are four basic attitudes towards life, or towards values, or towards ethics that do not need an extensive treatment. However they are real options of men of today and need a quick look.

(1) *Sociological determinism.* That there should be a science such as sociology is not challenged. Many of our present problems can be understood and helped by our modern expert knowledge of sociology. But there is a disease of the heart which sociologists suffer from and that is *sociological determinism.*

When a sociologist spends many years in specialized reading and much actual field survey, it is very easy for him to come to the conclusion that mankind is gripped and controlled by the social context. Man's morals, his values, his religion, his pastimes, etc., are dictated to him by his society. In the study of crime or juvenile delinquency or dope addiction he sees people over and over and over again as helpless pawns of larger sociological forces. It is not difficult for him to become a believer in *sociological determinism.*

The Christian does not challenge a great deal of what the sociologist affirms. Much he thinks is a reflection of biblical truth itself. But the Christian wants to say there is some area of free choice left as small as it may be. Sociological forces are not irresistible like the Calvinistic doctrine of irresistible grace. Nor do we agree that ethics can be completely reduced to social custom (mores). That is to say right and wrong can never be totally matters of custom, tradition, or sociological environment. There is an area in each man's life where there is an unsharable responsibility even in the presence of the strongest of sociological forces. And therefore no man can totally excuse himself on the basis of sociological determinism. No matter how small that negotiable territory is, it is there.

(2) *Humanism.* Originally humanism was a declaration of freedom from a life governed totally by the church, or totally by concerns of salvation and the world to come. It defended the basic integrity of values in this life and on this earth and values and occupations that

77

were worthwhile even though not religious. This was certainly a healthy humanism.

However, humanism eventually changed its face. If "clericalism" was an interpretation of life that was purely religious and denied the real meaning of the doctrine of creation, humanism erred on the other side and said that the *only* life is this life, the *only* values are now values, the *only* goods are this life's goods.

The respect the humanists give to the doctrine of creation (even though they do not know that this is what they are doing) is correct. Their denial of human destiny, of eternal life, and the real meaning of faith in God, and of an order that transcends this present order is wrong and the Christian ethicist must challenge it.

Humanism is the functional religion and the functional ethics of intellectuals. On the one hand they believe that Christianity, its theology and its ethics, can no longer be believed by modern man. Yet they cannot resign themselves to the vision of Bertrand Russell in his earlier years who pictured the universe as a vast machine totally indifferent to man and swallowing him up into oblivion as eternal matter marched on. Rather, while denying ultimate or final answers to questions, mankind is to live as much as possible by ethical standards that attribute to man and his efforts a measure of dignity and worth. It is an ethics of the "as if."

In the past decade a Christian humanism has emerged. It has a skeptical side. The world of the future, the eschatological, cannot be known. Supernaturalism in Christianity is no longer possible so man does not know the future. Therefore the Christian faith, on its positive side, is a *now* faith. It is a faith of *this* world. Christian faith, Christian life, and Christian ethics are bounded by this now world. Therefore the only kind of ethic Christians can have is a Christian humanism.

(3) *Secularism.* The older secularism had a number of beliefs in common with humanism. It was essentially an assertion that the only world we know is this world, and the only values or standards for man were of this world. It therefore represented a stern denial of the theological and ethical system of Christianity.

As indicated it overlaps humanism. If any rule of the thumb distinction can be made it would be that humanism represents an effort to save the dignity of man apart from Christian theology. It has a humanitarian impulse. Secularism has been more an antireligious or anticlerical or antisupernatural philosophy. So understood it is roughly equivalent to atheism and its followers are to be counted in the millions.

But there has also emerged a so-called Christian secularism. This is hard to manage because there are many versions of Christian secularism. Perhaps the one thing they have in common is that Christian man knows this world; this is the world Jesus lived in; this is the world God created; and therefore the only viable Christian faith is a Christian secularism (i.e., Harvey Cox and the celebration of the secular). Or it may be argued that God is trying to put man on his own. God refuses to be man's perpetual crutch through the ages. Man has come of age, man knowing more of the construction of the cosmos than any previous generation, must now find his life, his meaning, his religion in a this-world context. His chief purpose is not to glorify God and enjoy him forever in a blessed eternity but to realize as much as one can the love of God revealed in Jesus in this present, here-and-now world of humanity (i.e., Bonhoeffer). Hence the only ethic for Christianity is a Christian secularism.

(4) *Nihilism.* Nihilism comes in two versions. To some nihilism is the final criticism of the culture of the West, the end of the old regime or synthesis. Some Russian political movements were called nihilistic and Nietzsche considered himself such a nihilist.

In the more popular meaning it is a denial of any meaning to life. It looks upon all ethical standards, religious beliefs, philosophical beliefs, or claims to truth to be either transient or spurious. That there have been people who have claimed to be nihilists is beyond argument. But that any person can really live a philosophy of nihilism is, at least on the psychological level, to be doubted. If nihilism is truth then it naturally follows that there is no truth at all in Christian values and Christian ethics.

IV

ETHICAL PROBLEMS OF THE CHRISTIAN AND THE CHURCH

Section 300: Birth Control

Crude methods to prevent the birth of children or to kill the fetus have been practiced at least since the times of the Greeks and the Romans. Birth control by the use of chemicals or scientifically designed devices is relatively recent. Furthermore the reasons for or against such practices have become far more articulate and sophisticated.

Birth control is not equivalent to birth elimination. It is the case that birth control methods have been used to prevent any children from being born but that is not the essential idea of birth control. Furthermore the general problem of procreation is not new to this generation of the Christian church but the discussions began in the patristic period. However, our concern here is not historical but rather to present an analysis of the situation for the present century.

Birth control as practiced among Protestants is usually defended on three grounds:

(1) Birth control allows for the proper spacing of children. When children are born in rapid succession an enormous amount of physical and psychological strain is put on the mother. The continuous inflation of doctors' fees and hospital fees is a more recent stress of a financial nature. Some women can readily handle the stresses of having children come in the so-called stepladder pattern. But to other women it is a strain beyond their physical and emotional resources to handle.

It is not uncommon for some kind of neurosis or other emotional disturbance to be precipitated by a steady succession of births. By the use of birth control methods the physical, emotional, and financial stresses can be so moderated that the stresses do not become damaging or unmanageable. The proper spacing of children prevents this.

It is also known that families that space their children have fewer problems in general and far happier home environments.

(2) Birth control enables a couple to set a reasonable limit to the size of their family. *This is the stewardship of children.* It means that no couple should have more children than they can properly feed, house, clothe, educate and give proper dental and medical care. When a couple produces more children than they can adequately manage in the terms just stated, trouble begins. Children are not properly fed nor clothed nor educated nor cared for dentally, medically, and emotionally. When this happens the sociological problems pile up as well as the medical and the psychological ones. To bring a child into the world when he cannot get the basic things he needs for his well-being is considered a wrong against the child. What is a reasonable number of children cannot be fixed but something determined by each family situation.

(3) Birth control is necessary where there are either physical conditions or psychological conditions existing which make the birth of a child a very dangerous matter. Women with severe physical problems can have another child only at the risk of their own lives. Sometimes the neurotic or psychotic or genetic factors of either the mother or the father simply spell tragedy if another child is born.

(4) The fact that the human race is going through a population explosion is common knowledge. If present conditions persist, the human race will eventually run out of land, food, and air. The present increase of population is 65 million people a year. By the year 2000 A.D. world population will be pushing hard towards the seven billion mark.

There is a good deal of speculation now going on in which scientists are trying to cope with the food problem. For example, the present intake of 55 million tons of fish per year from the ocean can be raised to 200 million tons. But that in turn creates other problems with sea life so that it is not a simple solution. Experiments are being made to develop wheat and rice that double or triple ordinary yield. Chemical farms built in forms of skyscrapers is another speculation. Others hope that atomic war might bring the population back to reasonable numbers or that the impact of the sheer number of people will kill the sex drive. It is not right to say that it is impossible for man to solve the food problem for ten billion people. But at the present way in which food is produced and at the present rate of population growth a great tragedy is in the making. World-wide birth control is the most realistic solution.

On the other hand a number of objections have been made against birth control:

(1) It can be psychologically damaging. No method of birth control is one hundred percent effective. The severing of the vas deferens in the male and the tying up of the Fallopian tubes in the female are the most nearly perfect means of birth control. Side effects of the pill are now being reported. This means that a number of women still suffer tension, anxiety, and other destructive emotions.

(2) Birth control can be used by a couple who are essentially selfish and avoid children in favor of their own independence.

(3) There is the apprehension that the people who practice birth control are the more intelligent of the race, and the people who do not are the poorer specimens. Unintentionally birth control could constantly decrease the number of gifted children born and increase those with an inferior genetic heritage.

(4) The chief reason for sexuality in nature and man is the procreation of the race. Birth control is thus violation of natural law. The Roman Catholic church has been strongest at this point. But recent studies of Roman Catholic families by external experts and articles by highly informed Roman Catholic scholars indicate that the traditional Catholic position is breaking up. Whatever the statements are from the officials of the Roman Catholic church, the practice of Roman Catholic doctors and Roman Catholic couples is contrary to the teachings of the Magisterium and more like that of enlightened Protestants.

In the Protestant-Catholic dialogue on marriage the Roman Catholic position has been that the function of human sexuality is for the bearing of children and resort is made to Genesis 1 for scriptural proof. The Protestant position has been that marriage is first for fellowship or companionship and then for procreation. The appeal is made to Genesis 2 where God creates a companion for Adam. There are now a few Roman Catholic scholars who show sympathy for the Protestant view because it presents a sounder psychological and spiritual foundation for marriage than marriage conceived of as primarily for the production of children.

However, this is not the traditional Roman Catholic position on this problem. A Roman Catholic couple is not bound to have as many children as possible. They may exercise restraint (brother-sister or Joseph-Mary relationships) or they may follow the rhythm method. Or, they do not consider it contrary to their teaching if in treating one medical problem the secondary result is that the woman cannot become pregnant.

To complete the picture it must be confessed that many very conservative Protestant groups have views about marriage and birth control that are virtually identical to the Roman Catholic position.

A problem bordering on birth control although somewhat different is forced celibacy. By forced celibacy we mean that there are people who for various reasons cannot marry, or if they marry sexual relations are not possible.

Some people are born deformed or through disease or accident cannot have normal sexual experiences (even though they can marry). Some people are not asked to be married by a member of the other sex, or else they have found it impossible to find that person whom they felt would make an acceptable life partner. The birth rate of boys and girls vary. It is always plus or minus 50 percent (but the variation is never more than 2 percent) so that there will always be extra boys or extra girls. Dangerous occupations, wars, and pioneering are all ways of killing a number of men so that the male-female balance gets out of proportion. In fact after a major world war the number of women who will never marry because of the dead on the battlefield and the crippled in the hospital runs into the millions.

It must be confessed that there is very little Scripture on this difficult subject. Both Christ and Paul indicated that some people had enough sainthood to forego marriage and sexuality (Matt. 19:12, 1 Cor. 7:7). But the number of people without this heroic grace is very many, and what is to be said to them? Paul is at least realistic enough to admit that sexual passion is a major force in the race and needs some control (1 Cor. 7:9).

As indicated there is no Scripture or body of Scripture that clarifies this problem. The only real theological answer one is given is to pray for grace to endure celibate existence for God does have special grace for a kind of life that does call for heroic virtue. A psychologist may suggest sublimation (turning one's energies into some other direction so that the sex drive is moderated enough to be tolerated) as the solution to forced celibacy. We can at least express a hope that someday a more perfect understanding of human nature will provide the church with a realistic solution to this problem.

The more significant elements of medicals and morals (including a discussion of suicide) are treated in Joseph Fletcher, *Morals and Medicine* (contraception, artificial insemination, sterilization, and euthanasia). It must be remembered that this book was written *before* Fletcher's works on situation ethics.

Section 301: Divorce

From the earliest days of the Christian church to the present divorce has been a main concern of Christian ethics. Our problem is to investigate the divorce problem as it now is. The most obvious factor is the enormous increase in divorces in the past few decades. In California there are now as many divorces per year as marriages and this is indicative of the general increase of divorces in all states.

What does this inflation of divorces mean? To some it is a sign of a decadent civilization. To others it is a sign that our present marriage system is no longer relevant to modern society and some new pattern is in the making. To others it is a sign that people are now more honest. When they realize that a marriage is a mistake they do not senselessly continue it creating more psychological damage all the way around.

The particular causes of the inflation of divorce are known. Modern states now grant divorces for seven or eight reasons in contrast to the one historically sanctioned cause of adultery. Further these seven or eight new bases for divorce can be given very liberal interpretations.

We are now in the period of the "quickie" divorce. Some states have shortened the period of residency which qualifies a person as a member of that state which has a very easy and slack divorce system. Typical states that do this are Nevada, Florida, Idaho, Arkansas, Utah, and Alabama. Mexican divorces account for one-third of the divorces in America.

Sociologists have investigated divorce and marriage in great detail. They have a fairly clear picture of the divorce pattern. They know, for example, the kinds of marriages which are weak ones and usually end in divorce. The basic factor is this: *any marriage which crosses a major division in society is a weak marriage.* By a "weak" marriage they mean a marriage that has a high risk for ending in divorce. Rich-poor marriages, interracial marriages, and interreligious marriages are examples of high risk marriages for they cross a major division in society.

Through research, psychiatrists are also able to detemine what psychological elements make a marriage that will most likely end up in the divorce court. For example, people who have inadequate self-images of their own sexuality have fragile marriages that can easily pull apart.

The result on the total population because of this increased knowledge of the causes for divorce is a more tolerant attitude toward divorce. Divorce is thought of less and less as a moral or religious question and more and more as a sociological and psychological problem. Be that as it may, divorce is still a major ethical problem in the Christian church.

(1) *The Roman Catholic Church.* The Roman Catholic church considers marriage a sacrament if its participants have been baptized in the name of the Father, Son, and Holy Spirit. As a sacrament it can never be undone. There is no divorce of any kind in the Roman Catholic church. It does however, permit separation of bed and board (*mensa et thoro*).

Christ seems to grant grounds for divorce on the basis of adultery (Matt. 19:9). The Roman Catholic church has a special interpretation of *porneia,* adultery. To them it means a defective marriage. The so-called Pauline privilege (1 Cor. 7:15) is also a defective marriage. Defective marriages may be annulled. All so-called divorce cases are reviewed by the bishop's office in each diocese. The divorce is pronounced as a divorce and therefore contrary to Roman Catholic canon law; or it is declared a defective marriage and annulled. But if the person or persons involved think that justice has not been done they may appeal to a special institution at Rome known as the Rota. To date the policy of the Rota has been very conservative.

The no-divorce rule creates problems special to Roman Catholics. It encourages, unintentionally of course, common-law marriages. If such a couple breaks up it is not a divorce and they are still in communion with the Roman Catholic church. It also inadvertently creates a double standard. When a man feels frustrated in his marriage he may maintain the outward appearance of a marriage but have a liaison with a mistress.

(2) *The Strict Protestant View.* Historically most denominations in the Protestant camp have had views very similar to those in Roman Catholicism but with one difference. They believe that Matthew 19:9 and 1 Corinthians 7:15 allow for legal divorce but deny any remarriage. No other causes for divorce are countenanced. However the ban against remarriage has not been universal for some of the older Protestant ethicists felt that the innocent party had a right to remarry.

(3) *The Broad Protestant Principle.* The assumption of the strict Protestant view which seldom if ever is deliberately stated is that the New Testament gives us *all* the essential ethical guides for divorce. The broad Protestant position believes that the New Testament gives the church the fundamentals of Christian marriage, and the very serious aggravations which may be solved only by divorce. It does not believe that the New Testament gives the church any exhaustive treatment of the subject but to the contrary, the very minimum of treatment. It accuses the ethicists who hold to a very strict view of divorce of being naïve or unrealistic in facing the thousands of facts we now know about marriage and divorce from medicine, psychology, and sociology.

Richard S. Soulen has shown that an examination of the texts in the New Testament about divorce reveal not a uniform teaching but a struggle of the early church to come to terms with the complexities of divorce dating from the very earliest days of the Christian church ("Marriage and Divorce: A Problem in New Testament Interpretation," *Interpretation,* October, 1969). This should serve as a caution to any who want to make a simple (and unrealistic) codification of what the New Testament says about divorce.

With our modern sociological and psychological knowledge of marriage and divorce the church must come to some new thinking about divorce, especially fundamentalist churches that perpetuate marriage patterns of previous centuries that are now unrealistic. Some of the added factors that must be considered in rethinking divorce are:

(1) *Impotency.* Impotency is the failure of either male or female to engage completely in the sex act. In the man it is premature ejaculation or the inability to have an erection. With a woman it is the impossibility of coming to orgasm. This problem is far more prevalent than the average Christian layman or pastor realizes and creates very serious problems in marriage. It is recognized in some states as grounds for divorce. We cannot offer medical or psychological advice at this point. Our point is that if the church is going to deal realisti-

cally with the modern divorce problem it must come to terms with the problem of impotency and what factor it may be in the divorce problem. Certainly medical and psychological advice should be sought.

(2) *Minors.* In most states marriage by minors is legal only by consent of parents. Yet there is no word of this problem in Scripture. The church must resort to the best information it can get from sociology and psychology on this problem in forming its own attitude toward the marriage of minors.

(3) *Alcohol.* People may marry under the influence of alcohol or drugs or narcotics. Or one of the couple may have a serious neurotic or psychotic problem that has been masked during courtship. There are alcoholics or alcoholic dependent persons that marry. There are homosexuals who marry to conceal their homosexuality. Most states allow automatic divorce if either of the couple is sentenced to prison for ten years or more. Here again none of these matters are specified in Scripture yet the Christian church must deal with these problems for they very realistically enter into the ethics of marriage and divorce.

The Christian pastor who thinks that the New Testament contains an exhaustive ethics of marriage and divorce is at a loss to handle the kinds of problems he now faces in society. Rather than thinking through to a more relevant ethic of marriage and divorce he resigns the case to the decision of the court and continues his simplistic views in preaching and counseling. The right way is to strive for a *total* Christian ethic of marriage and divorce so that the church has an ethic for all possible cases and doesn't resign the hard ones to the decision of the court. Christian ethics should have principles that do deal realistically with these difficult cases and thankfully it is doing so more and more.

To state it bluntly, evangelical and conservative churches back away from the really complex issues in divorce. They do not seem to be able to cope with the modern divorce problem save in a legalistic manner which many times results in cruel decisions or attitudes. They must no longer evade the complexities of the modern divorce problem but must attempt to have a total Christian ethic where the hard cases as well as the obvious cases are given Christian interpretation and Christian guidance. The Christian who wants a total Christian ethic tries to include these difficult problems in his basic ethics and attempts some kind of Christian solution rather than willy-nilly turning such cases over to civil law.

Parenthetically it may be observed that some churches have canon law or its equivalent and these cases can be handled uniformly within the given church community. Churches that have no such regulatory means attempt to solve such cases on a purely individualistic basis depending on the opinions of the pastor or the local congregation.

There is another important element in the broader Christian ethic about divorce and that is the attempt to solve some of these wretchedly complex cases by a spirit of love, of understanding, and of redemption. Such an ethic attempts to work the best it can within Christian presuppositions of knowledge about divorce gained from sociologists, psychologists, doctors, and lawyers. The attempt is to salvage or redeem life rather than to treat people in a strict, moralistic, and legalistic manner.

It is common knowledge with psychologists that a bad marriage is psychologically destructive. It creates bitter, hostile, and unforgiving attitudes in the couple. It may work all sorts of psychological damage on the children. To maintain a destructive marriage on the basis of being loyal to a Christian ethic of no divorce is hardly justifiable. Love, justice, mercy, and redemption are ground underfoot to preserve a moralistic view. If a pastor does not believe in divorce, in many of these cases he should at least be ready to advise separation of bed and board.

Each case has to be settled in terms of its own configuration of factors. There is little that rules can do in such unique situations. The only rule is really the rule of redemption: the church ought to follow ethical policies that are redemptive, that are healing, that offer hope for happiness in the future, and that do not intend to harm or hurt people simply to comply with the ethics of their "in group."

Remarriage of people with unfortunate marriages that have been terminated by divorce must become a matter of great concern to the Christian church because the present inflation of divorce rates crosses deeply into Christian territory. Paul says that human beings burn with sexual passion (1 Cor. 7:9), and that one of the functions of marriage is to keep sexual passion within moral boundaries.

But what message has the Christian church to those people who as normal people do have sexual passions? A divorced person does not suddenly become asexual. The possibility of people, Christian or non-Christian, who have been divorced and not remarried to become promiscuous is rather high. And regardless of what the Roman Catholic church says, very few Christians have the heroism or saintliness to remain celibate through many decades of life. Sticking hard to a traditional Christian ethic in these difficult cases may soothe our churchified conscience but we have done *nothing* for the person in this most difficult predicament.

For a young person to be divorced and to remain celibate the rest of his life is indeed a form of heroism. But there is another facet to this problem even more disturbing. Children need father and mother figures with whom to identify psychologically. In normal home life girls identify with mother and boys with father. Some of the saddest cases a counselor has to face are those where a child has not been able to make a proper identification. A divorced home where there are children becomes a split home. The problem of identification becomes very serious. It is for this reason that so many problem adults stem from divorced homes. As a simple rule of the psychology of personality development, boys need fathers and girls need mothers and divorces tragically break up this necessary pattern. Certainly not all children from divorced homes end up neurotic or as criminals. Many other factors may come into existence to prevent it. However, remarriage is one of the better solutions.

Therefore our Protestant churches need a new sense of compassion, a new sense of mercy, a new sense of redemption, and need to make a real effort at understanding the tragedy of divorce. Every effort should be made to redeem these people, and open up doors of hope for them rather than plunging them into deeper despair or deeper problems.

There are three dangers in any attempt to take a more generous view of the problem of divorce and remarriage.

(1) Any concession for a worthy case is capitalized upon by an endless number of unworthy persons. The special concession for an aggravated case is turned into an excuse by people whose situation is not aggravated.

(2) People who are divorced frequently remarry the same kind of person they married the first time and soon have a record of two divorces. A great number of divorced people never learn the psychological dynamics that broke up their first marriage so they perpetuate their error in the second marriage and therefore remarriage is no solution at all for such people.

(3) Every divorce has a tragic element in it. People do not walk

out of each other's lives. The persons, the problems, and the financial and property matters involved in the divorce do not suddenly evaporate when the divorce is granted. Heartaches, bad feelings, a sense of loneliness, attacks of anger, spells of anxiety, and a continuous rehashing of the past keep on going long after the formal separation. Divorce and remarriage may settle some very big problems, but not all the fires are burned out and these fires can smolder for years. So any couple contemplating divorce must realize that the legal end of a marriage and the emotional ending of a marriage are two very different things and to think that they both happen at the same time is part of the tragedy of the divorce phenomenon.

Section 302: Abortion

It is impossible to get reliable statistics on the number of abortions in America each year. Abortions recognized as proper medical procedure for therapeutic reasons number about 200,000. The number of abortions performed in various forms of disguises or illegal abortions or Mexican abortions could run the figure up close to 2,000,000 a year. Some estimates are sure that it is at least as high as 1,500,000.

One would be very naïve not to believe that a good number of these abortions involve girls who are members of Christian churches. Abortion is then not a problem of the nonchurched alone, but is an issue that must be discussed in Christian ethics.

When is a person a person? when does a fetus cease to be a tissue and become a person? etc., etc., are somewhat academic questions in spite of the very high emotions that still color such discussions. That is not where the real issues are. The real issue is why should *any* woman in the twentieth century want an abortion? Why should any Christian girl want an abortion? Here is where the discussion must start. Until the actual picture is seen the debate is going to be unrealistic and academic.

(1) In the rare case when a woman is raped and becomes pregnant she may want an abortion. This is especially compelling if the woman has been raped by a person of another race. In our larger colleges where there is a mixture of races there are a number of abortions each year not on the basis of rape but simply on the basis of pregnancies resulting from intercourse between couples of different races.

90

(2) It is not uncommon for an older relative to intimidate or seduce a younger female relative and the girl become pregnant. An abortion seems to be the best resolution of this rather nasty relationship created within a circle of relatives.

(3) A girl who is a minor may give consent to sexual intercourse and feel justified in having an abortion if she becomes pregnant on the basis that she gave consent before she was legally responsible.

(4) A woman who has a family already too large to manage may feel it justifiable to have an abortion. Women with a high resistance to the idea of an abortion at the time of their marriage usually reverse their position after the birth of the fifth child.

(5) Illicit relationships may end in pregnancy and an abortion in another city or state seems the most reasonable solution to a complicated problem.

(6) Neurotic or psychotic women can be pushed deeper into their emotional illness if they give birth to a child and an abortion prevents the deepening of the neurosis or psychosis.

(7) Exhaustive studies have been made on how many diseases are inherited. For example, Huntington's chorea is inherited. There is no cure for it. The person's nervous system begins an irreversible process of degeneration. Abortion seems to be the only humane means of preventing another case of Huntington's chorea. Geneticists are collecting extensive files on diseases to determine how many of them are hereditary. When they have determined the diseases that are hereditary, then some measures—either birth control or abortion—must be taken to prevent further tragic births.

(8) The large cities and counties of America are faced with the problem of rapidly expanding relief rolls. The obvious answer seems to be to limit the size of many of these families through birth control. Unless a person knows the problems a social worker faces at this point he has no idea of the dimensions of the problem. Thousands of people on relief rolls are so ignorant or so uneducated or so mentally deficient that the simplest birth control measures are neither followed nor understood. As one social worker put it, there are situations where birth control would not be practiced if one whole wall of the bedroom was an immense diagram and the other wall contained instructions in headliner print. The sheer pressure of the problem might force cities and counties into programs of sterilization or abortion as extreme as such a solution seems now.

91

We are not going to debate the Roman Catholic view about abortion. Except for very unusual cases where the life of the fetus is taken as part of a larger more complex surgical operation, the Roman Catholic church still considers abortion a form of homicide. It is our speculation that as the Roman Catholic church finds that it must moderate its position in so many things to stay a viable church in the modern world, it will eventually make some concessions here.

What does need to be pointed out is that two major intellectual revolutions have gone on in the past four hundred years.

(1) Modern medicine tends to treat its problems more and more as medical problems and less and less as theological or philosophical problems. Thus to abort or not to abort is seen within the total complex of the practice of medicine and decisions are made on this basis and not on a philosophical or theological one. This revolution has not spared the Roman Catholic church. Roman Catholic doctors are known by means of various polls to be practicing medicine more and more in terms of the larger common medical practice than according to the strict medical theology of the Roman Catholic church.

There is the possibility of a misunderstanding here. It may seem that doctors consider abortion as purely a physiological problem. That is not so. There is always a *psychological* reaction of a woman to abortion. In almost every case some kind of residual guilt eventually comes to the surface. The anticipated psychological effects on the woman are as much a consideration as are the physiological considerations. No responsible doctor would perform an abortion if the psychiatrist were to advise him that the abortion would push the woman into a deep psychotic depression or unrelievable feelings of guilt.

(2) A real theological change has come to pass since the Reformation. That is the Protestant conviction that man as lord of nature is to master and control nature. This means not only putting chemical fertilizer on the fields, changing the courses of rivers, building dams, harvesting forests, developing chemicals of all sorts, developing education and the sciences, but also a new attitude towards medicine. Man is now to be lord of his body as he is of nature. Therefore many of the attitudes about the human body developed by the theologians in the patristic and medieval periods are no longer relevant to the modern Protestant. And this influences how he feels about abortion.

The Protestant develops his thinking within newer contexts and debates with Roman Catholics may be interesting but not fruitful.

There are three prevailing theories about abortion:

(1) There should never be an abortion, except perhaps in grave cases where some serious matter such as a spreading cancer is concerned. This is not just a Roman Catholic position. Some Protestants believe that life is life from God and no matter how the life has come into existence man has no right to end it. Amputating a leg and aborting a fetus are two different matters. The refusal to abort expresses the uniqueness of life as given of God.

A second reason is that abortion always leaves a psychological scar. Although some women may bear it easier than others, none escape the psychological damage. In fact the damage may be potentially so great that it is best to treat all cases as if the damage might be maximum. The feelings of a woman and new life in her body are among the deepest of all human feelings and therefore must be treated with maximum regard, honor, and caution.

(2) There should be abortion on request. The Russian government did announce such a policy. In 1921, 21 percent of the Russian women who became pregnant requested abortion. In 1926, 90 percent requested abortion. Needless to say the law was changed. Both Japan and Sweden are noted for their generous laws about abortion but still there are regulations so that the Russian phenomenon will not be repeated. Abortion by request is, of course, the most liberal view there is of abortion and some feel the only enlightened view but as the Russian experiment showed, it could result in internal genocide.

(3) The one accepted position today is the therapeutic abortion. Ordinarily this has been restricted to cases of medical complications. However, it is now being enlarged to include psychological complications. In responsible hospitals all potential cases of abortion are matters of team decision where the whole picture of the patient is set forth from the social worker to the surgeon.

Before we conclude this discussion a few more observations are in order:

(1) There is a common census of opinion that if the fetus cannot live outside the mother it is still tissue and not person; if it can live outside the mother (as in a premature birth) it is to be considered a person and not a tissue. This is virtually going back to Plato who said that a baby is not a person until it is born.

(2) There is a common concensus that if a decision is to be made either for the mother or the fetus the decision should be in favor of

the mother who is a known person as against the fetus which is as yet an unknown quantity (which is opposite to Roman Catholic opinion).

(3) Abortion is not a mandatory solution. The child may be born and adopted out if that is necessary or kept by the mother if she wishes. The situation is not always a forced issue to abort or not to abort.

(4) The matter of guilt, if this is a factor, must be seen as corporate. A young girl becoming pregnant is usually the result of a complex of factors in which a number of people contribute to the situation. To place all guilt on the pregnant girl is preeminently unfair.

(5) There is no Protestant view as such about abortion. There is a growing concensus of Protestants about abortion. For example, there should be no abortion until the medical facts, the psychological facts, the family facts, and the sociological facts are known. Policies about when to abort and when not to abort should be governed as much by the experiences of the past with abortion as well as theological elements. The weight of the past—too much ethics about medical matters were made in the Christian church prior to modern medicine— must not prejudice present opinions about abortion. Decisions about abortion should be reviewed as decisions about all matters, namely, redemptively. What is the most redemptive action for this woman's life? Redemption looks for a life of happiness and not of misery. Christians must take a second think if their decisions are going to increase misery and evil and suffering and harm even though they think their opinion is ethically the right one. Mercy should conquer justice.

Section 303: Medicine and Death

There are thousands of people in America today living what can be called only a living death. Besides what happens in daily life the Viet Nam War is creating its terrible number of soldiers whose condition can only be described as living death. One powerful injection can end this vegetable existence forever.

Many of these cases are kept alive by physiological machines. If the person were left to himself he would die. But he is kept alive as a human vegetable through machines.

As one begins to research the implications of these living vegetables, "gorks" as they are called, he runs into frustration upon frustration.

It is a depressing experience to walk through the wards of institutions that keep such people alive. None will ever walk again; many will never again recognize the face of a loved one; many will never again have a conscious moment. None will ever again be part of the family circle or the family conclave during a holiday season. What should modern society do with the living dead? In other generations these people would have long ago gone to be with their Maker. Do we have a right to postpone the inevitable in the name of science for it is hardly in the name of mercy?

(1) *The mood of society.* The Christian tradition from the inception of the church is that human life has a sacredness that animals do not have. The modern Christian is struggling with this problem: Can human suffering and sickness reach a point where the concept of the sacredness of life becomes meaningless? Modern medicine seems to indicate that there is such a limit. But at present both in the church and outside the church the concept of the sacredness of life remains unchanged, namely, human life is human life and is to be maintained at all costs and at all odds. Until this mood changes, talks about euthanasia (easing a hopeless case into death) or anti-dysthanasia (protesting the perpetuation of life by all possible medical means thus extending the time, pain, and misery of dying) are going to be academic and fruitless.

Patients, relatives, and doctors will experience *frustration* until society rethinks what it means to be a person, what value it attaches to maintaining life even at its lowest possible level, and what is the ethical justification of spending enormous sums of money on hopeless cases while redeemable cases go untreated because of lack of funds.

(2) *The rules.* Already the medical society is working in teams and forming rules as they go as in the case of therapeutic abortion. But when it comes to forming rules about life itself one runs into frustration. No single person nor group of persons seems wise enough to form rules that cannot be abused. There are those who doubt if such rules should even exist. Yet here again is frustration. Case after case seems to require something new in medical ethics yet the problems of bringing forth that new ethic seem insurmountable. Someday the rules will come but until then we must live with our frustrations.

(3) *The stewardship of money.* Tens of thousands of dollars are spent daily keeping human vegetables alive. In the meantime there are millions of children in desperate need of every kind of medical

help. Here again we face a deep frustration. It is wrong to spend thousands upon thousands of dollars on persons who are but inches from death, and let children suffer for lack of funds. As impotent as society now seems to reverse this situation, in the name of humanity it must be reversed. Again until that day of reversal comes we live with frustration.

(4) *Guilt feelings.* Relatives do not always treat each other with the full respect they each require. Yet when an elderly relative becomes sick to the point where recovery is impossible, the relatives suddenly experience deep feelings of guilt. They feel that the years they have neglected their loved one must now be atoned for. So they demand heroic efforts from doctors and hospitals to keep the loved one alive. Here again is frustration.

While this elderly person is hopelessly sick there may be other youngsters in the same community going untreated through lack of funds. Is it right for large sums to be spent on the living dead and let others go neglected? Here again there is the feeling of frustration. Someday, perhaps too long in the future, we will come to the point where we get our values in proper order and expend our sums for those who can be helped rather than wasting them on people beyond any reasonable hope of recovery.

(5) *Law suits.* Unfortunately suing doctors for malpractice is on a sharp increase. Rates for insurance against malpractice are doubling and tripling. If a doctor is confronted with a hopeless case and he does nothing, he may expose himself to a suit. He therefore does all he can with modern medicine knowing he is fighting a losing battle. It is the only way he can prevent a law suit. Here again is frustration when medicine must be practiced for purely legal protection and not for the real character of the case.

It will take decades to relieve medical practice of some of these frustrations. Fortunately it is not all this bad. Conferences of mutual trust among doctors and patients and relatives are relieving some of these frustrations.

Section 304: Funeral Practices

There is continuous unrest among Christian theologians and pastors concerning the moral discrepancy between the cost of the burial of a human body and the worth of a corpse. The rub is between the amount of money spent for the disposing of the body and the worth of the body. Or to state it differently, what is the right stewardship of money regarding the worth of a dead body and the amount of money spent in funeral costs, flowers, graves, and headstones?

(1) There is something wrong with our whole set of values when the cost of disposing of a deceased person is usually more than bringing life into the world. In the first instance there is no real gain to society or civilization or the significant alleviation of human misery, whereas with the birth of a child there is the beginning of a new personality and a new life. When the "negative" is more expensive than the "positive," some serious ethical rethinking must be done.

(2) The sales policies involved in funerals have been subjected to careful analysis, and such practices are found to show considerable lack of integrity for the deceased family. One cannot, of course, generalize and say all directors of funeral parlors conduct the same kind of confusing practices.

However, it is common practice to follow sales procedures that confuse the family in its decisions rather than to help it. The purchase of the casket determines the basic cost of the funeral. Therefore the sales methods in selling the casket are designed to confuse the customer so that he cannot really "shop" for a casket. For example, the priest or rabbi or minister is separated from the family at the time of casket selection if this can be managed. This is unfortunate because these men are experienced and could give seasoned advice to the family.

In the citation of prices the family is told dollar differences between caskets and not the total price. This makes real comparison of costs confusing. Some funeral directors have an established circuit through the display room of caskets calculated to induce the family to buy a casket not too many dollars less than the original expensive casket they first rejected. Studies of funeral practices have shown that similar sharp practices are involved in the sale of flowers, grave sites, and markers.

That a person should be buried with dignity is beyond question. That at a time of grief and confused judgment a family should be subjected to unusually clever sales techniques is hardly ethical.

(3) A further concern in Christian ethics is the services or items sold that amount to sheer financial exploitation: giving the family the impression that embalming is a state law when this is not universally

the case; selling expensive caskets with oil paintings on the inside for the contemplation of the dead person; selling expensive burial garments when the deceased's own clothes are adequate; or selling caskets with elaborate interior materials so that the deceased will rest easier. Again, one cannot generalize and affirm that all funeral directors carry on such practices. But certainly a concerned Christian ethic would assert that selling such meaningless items to a family in its time of bereavement and confusion is not ethical.

(4) The exploitation of the grief of the bereaved family is another matter of ethical concern. A funeral parlor should be a business concern which helps people through one of the most painful experiences of life. The grief of people in this situation should not be a point of advantage in sales pressure by the funeral director.

(5) Attempts to avoid being subjected to such shrewd policies are difficult. Giving one's body to science is a solution for a few people. There are cooperative burial associations but these usually are found only in the larger cities. Cremation is usually cheaper than burial but still a great deal of "pagan feeling" is associated with cremation.

We have tried to indicate the abuses in the funeral practices which we feel are not consistent with the Christian attitude towards the shell of the former person. There are many firms of real integrity and there are a number of Christian people in the funeral business. And the cost of many items are beyond the immediate control of the funeral director. With all of these factors we have understanding and sympathy. We only protest those practices which amount to clever exploitation of people when grief blunts their better judgment and they are easy victims to shrewd and unethical practices.

Section 305: Tobacco

Historically speaking there has not been a uniform conviction about tobacco among Christians. Its approval or disapproval tended to follow regional and denominational lines. Recent medical research has now made the use of tobacco an ethical matter for all Christians.

If a person consistently smokes two or more packages of cigarettes a day, the chances are one out of five that he will get lung cancer. Or in terms of percentages 20 percent of such smokers get cancer of the lung. But this is only part of the story. Smoking has a bad systemic effect on the body. It can significantly raise blood pressure and aggravate heart trouble. It is also a contributing cause of emphysema—the inability of the lungs to absorb oxygen. Smoking a pipe may cause cancer of the tongue or lip.

If there is this much potential damage to the human body—and the research is by no means ended—then it seems that a Christian faces a real ethical decision in the use of tobacco. If the body is the temple of the Holy Spirit, and if good health is understood (other things being equal) as a Christian obligation, then the Christian response to tobacco should not be too difficult to decode.

Section 306: Christian Ethics and Alcohol

America is a *damp society*. This is the stubborn fact that every pastor, every Christian, and every church has to face. Any realistic discussion must begin here. A number of studies of alcohol usage in America have been made, and it is now known that 80 percent of the American people sometime in a given year will do some drinking. That is what is meant by America being a *damp society*. The figure 80 percent obviously includes millions of Christians. It refers to *all* alcoholic consumption, ranging from the confirmed alcoholic who drinks his bottle or two a day to the person who sips one or two cocktails at a social or business affair where everybody is expected to participate. The latter may constitute the individual's alcohol input for an entire year.

Many Christians think that the solution to the alcohol problem is prohibition or signing the pledge or requiring total abstinence. However studies in alcoholism show that this is an oversimplification of the problem. For example, to make a demand of an alcoholic that he immediately totally abstain from alcohol usually creates deep guilt feelings within him. Rather than driving him away from alcohol it drives him deeper into it. The suggested cure increases the disease. Alcoholism is a complicated psychological and medical problem and the Christian church must approach it from this angle. Supposedly simple Christian solutions may create problems rather than solve them.

The basic problem with alcohol is not hard to locate. It is a strong narcotic that can be freely purchased. Millions of Americans have emotional problems and stress situations at work and at home. The use of alcohol is the easiest and most direct way they have of working with their emotions and stresses. Any other drug that might help them, even though many degrees milder than alcohol, can be had only by prescription. So the doctor is passed up as the distressed person makes his way to the liquor store. In short, alcohol is an open market, do-it-yourself psychological kit for millions of Americans.

The physiological effect of alcohol is very dangerous. It goes directly to the *control tower* of the brain, that is, to the higher centers and begins a deadening effect. It lessens one's sense of judgment and co-ordination, and relaxes his inhibitions. Other narcotics usually work slower and on different parts of the brain.

The teaching of Holy Scripture on wine and hard liquor is not complicated. Wine has been used as a food for thousands of years in the Asiatic and European continents. It is placed on the table with other foods. In fact we have approval of wine in Holy Scripture as stated in Psalm 104:15, ". . . and wine to gladden the heart of man." Such texts as Luke 10:34 and 1 Timothy 5:23 indicate that wine was considered a medicine as well as a food. In general wine appears in Scripture as part of the daily food intake of the people and there is no judgment against it.

However, the ancients did know how to make liquor stronger than wine although not as strong as our distilled liquors. The use of this kind of drink is forbidden in Scripture. Also wine can make a person drunk and drunkenness is forbidden in Scripture. In some cases it may become a spiritual issue and Paul says that if it does he will not drink wine (Rom. 14:21).

When wine is taken as a food and usually weakened or diluted with water, it is a relatively harmless drink. It is mixed with food and sipped along with the entire meal and any harmful effect of alcohol is greatly reduced if not eliminated.

But when we jump the centuries to America the picture changes radically. Americans drink the wrong way for the wrong reasons. In fact this has been called "the American way of drinking." It specializes in the hard liquors. Alcohol is gulped or swallowed and not sipped. It is treated more as a drug than as a food. It is frequently taken on an empty stomach so that there is no buffering or diluting effect of food. The drinker gets the full punch of the alcohol. It is frequently used as a psychological crutch—a drink before meeting an important person, a drink before facing a difficult situation, a drink before an important sales opportunity, a drink before having to tell somebody some bad news, a drink to get through a boring party, etc., etc.

The medical profession knows that prohibition is not an option in a damp society. Therefore the concensus is that Americans be taught how to drink safely—for they will drink. *We are a damp society.* Typical of the approach to the situation is William T. Terhune, M.D., *The Safe Way to Drink: How To Prevent Alcohol Problems Before They Start.*

Terhune's book is very valuable for the pastor or lay Christian. It is written by an experienced psychiatrist but not in a technical, medical style. Terhune makes no concession to alcohol. What he does say is that Americans will drink. Therefore the only realistic option for the medical man is to tell Americans how to drink as harmlessly as possible. His book intends to teach how to control or minimize the effects of alcohol. He knows that it is a narcotic and a serious troublemaker in American society. Some of these troubles are:

(1) Out of every one hundred people who start drinking 6.5 percent will become alcoholics. At present there is no test which will reveal who those 6.5 percent people are. As long as there is indiscriminate use of alcohol there is going to be alcoholism. Perhaps the day may come when the potential alcoholic can be determined by physiological or psychological testing.

(2) In a technological society alcohol is a killer. By the present unsystematic method of checking on traffic deaths, at least 50 percent can be traced to alcohol. We do not know how high the figure would be if systematic checks were made on all accidents. This is just the figure where fatalities are concerned and does not touch the other millions of victims with broken bones, smashed internal organs, and lacerated faces.

There are no figures available but it is believed that the great number of crashes of private planes is due to the pilot having had a bout of drinking before taking off.

We know that pilots of commercial planes, drivers of buses and trains, military men with high responsibility all have to be alcoholically "dry" at least twenty-four hours before going on duty.

It has already been indicated why alcohol is a killer. The stomach "sponges" it right into the blood stream and it immediately goes to work on the higher centers of the brain destroying judgment and co-ordination. The liver neutralizes alcohol at a very slow rate (a little more than an ounce an hour) so the damaging effect of alcohol is almost immediate and in the most important part of the brain.

To indicate the influence of alcohol on the brain some medical schools will give students a test on one day. Then the next day they will give them a similar test of the same difficulty after drinking a bottle of beer. The students report that the second test was easier and that they scored higher. Actually their scores drop 17 percent.

(3) Crime and immorality are increased by the use of alcohol. Our respectable social behavior is due to the inhibitions we have about doing certain things. It is not uncommon for criminals to do some drinking before they commit a crime so that they won't lose their nerve which by retranslation means that they dampen out their normal inhibitions. People who are ordinarily quite proper in their sexual behavior may become very free in their sexual responses after drinking because again the usual inhibitions have been dampened by alcohol.

(4) The use of alcohol can create alcohol dependency and alcoholism. At this point we come to a boundary line between ethics and medicine because we are not exactly sure where control is left behind and where drinking has become compulsive. In the beginning drinking is an ethical problem. If a person moves through alcohol dependency to alcoholism, he has become a psychiatric case. Alcohol counseling is complicated business. For those who wish to know more about it we suggest H. Clinebell's *Understanding and Counseling the Alcoholic.*

Before a person starts drinking and faces the possibility of becoming an alcoholic dependent or even an alcoholic, he should have some idea of the trouble he is asking for. Typical problems of alcohol dependency and alcoholism are:

(1) Alcohol is expensive and therefore heavy drinking can create real problems with the family budget.

(2) Alcoholism ruins sexual relationships because a drunk husband is not appreciated as a sexual partner.

(3) Alcoholism can create personality disorders which can ruin the harmony that should prevail in a normal home life.

(4) Alcoholism creates hangovers. In California alone it is estimated that one billion dollars a year are lost on wages by people who are nursing a hangover.

(5) Alcoholism progressively destroys one's self-image and ego strength and from that alone comes a whole bag full of psychological problems.

(6) The steady use of alcohol usually intensifies any other ailment or disease from which a person is suffering. The drinking person increases the intensity of at least twenty-five other diseases by the use of alcohol.

(7) Alcohol potentiates other drugs and a mixture of alcohol and drugs can throw a person into a coma and even produce death.

(8) Alcohol is a narcotic and the temptation of people with emotional problems is to deaden their problems with alcohol rather than go through the painful process of facing their problems in order to resolve them. In short alcohol usage for psychological reasons keeps emotionally sick people away from the very people who can help them.

It is a common complaint that for all that has been said the modern business world revolves around the cocktail bar and to stay in business one has to stay with alcohol. For this dilemma we make three suggestions:

(1) A resourceful person need not feel trapped in a particular job. If he has the right skills and the ability to maneuver he can relocate so that he does not have to do business at the cocktail bar.

(2) Even if a person does feel trapped in a job which requires business transactions across the cocktail bar, he himself does not have to drink. He can learn two or three effective but polite ways of either avoiding drinking or drinking a nonalcoholic beverage.

(3) One young executive came home each night half done in with alcohol and decided that this was no way to go through life. So he substituted other kinds of activities with customers such as fishing, boating, golfing, bowling, sightseeing, and scenic drives. His sales actually increased. He found out that most of his customers preferred some good outdoor exposure to being cooped up in a bar for two or three hours.

We do not underestimate the pressures of the sales and business world, but there is no unalterable law of the Medes and Persians which says that business can run only on alcohol. Resourceful people can find other ways to keep civilization going and still earn a living.

Section 307: Christian Ethics and Drugs

Directors of evangelical camps for young people are having to send young people home for smoking pot at the Bible-conference grounds.

It is not completely unheard of for young people to leave an evening church service and end up at a pot party.

In some middle-class regions of our cities it is estimated that 80 percent of the young people have either experimented with pot or smoke it regularly. If the figure of 80 percent is correct, it means that a large number of children from Christian homes are included.

To follow through with some more statistics the lowest estimate of marijuana users in America is 5,000,000 people. Others estimate the number of users to be between 12 million and 20 million. Most of these people use this drug or another for a period of time and then give it up. It is estimated that there are 2,000,000 drug-dependents and about 100,000 real addicts. This is in contrast to the estimated 6,000,000 alcoholics in America. Furthermore although drug addiction or usage or dependency has been a youth phenomenon, it is becoming more and more an adult problem. One of the basic reasons people are turning to drugs rather than alcohol is the claim that alcohol turns one off whereas drugs turn one on.

To presume that the usage of drugs is found only among non-Christians or the non-church group is to be uninformed about what is going on. The problem of drugs is right in the center of the life of the church.

At present there are many research projects going on related to all aspects of drug usage. For a statement of the basic facts regarding what drugs are being used and their effects, there are two pamphlets written for nontechnical people: *A Community Mental Health Approach to Drug Addiction* and *Psychedelics and the College Student*.

Drugs have replaced alcohol among the younger generation but, of course, not completely. There is a specific reason why a drug is preferred to a drink. A drug gives a person a "trip." A "trip" is any kind of unusual mind-expanding experience and may be stimulated by music or literature as well as by drugs. But the kind of drugs used are basically the mind-expanding drugs. In mind-expansion a whole unusual set of inward processes are triggered. Colors are brighter, music is heavenly, the power of each sense becomes greatly increased, and the sense of the passage of time is greatly altered. There are many other elements in a trip but these are representative of what happens. Of course sometimes the trip produces bad experiences and this kind of trip is called a "bummer."

Alcohol is still used. In some instances the drug acts more powerfully if alcohol is also taken. Alcohol is also used to put the police off the track. The person using drugs can mask the fact with alcohol, and if he is apprehended by the police, it will be for the usage of alcohol with its minor penalties compared to the major penalties now imposed for the use of drugs.

Unfortunately the newer drugs have not been used long enough to know their long range effects. Furthermore it is difficult to get some of the drugs in the pure form necessary for scientifically controlled research. The United States Government is now growing its own marijuana so as to be able to chemically purify it and by so doing get accurate test data. There is not too much debate over the use of heroin because its powerful addictive effects are well known. It is also a well-known fact that "speed" really damages the internal organs. LSD damages the chromosomes of cells. But judgments about the effects of marijuana differ greatly and there are heated discussions on the subject on television and radio and in newspapers, journals, and magazines.

It is to be regretted that some individuals have taken it upon themselves to "scientifically" experiment with drugs. When it cannot lawfully be done in this country, these people go to countries where the drug is permitted and perform their experiments there. The results of such experiments have great news value and are used for propaganda purposes by those who want to justify the use of drugs. However the reports of such experiments are colored too much by rationalization and not enough by carefully controlled research.

Central to this inflationary use of drugs is the question of *why*. Why has the drug replaced in the life of the young person the glass of beer, the hamburger, or the cigarette?

(1) One of the first justifications that one encounters is that it is the only kind of escape possible (even though for just a few hours) from all the misery, poverty, and depression of the blighted areas of our big cities. For a few hours the wretchedness of poverty can be forgotten in the fantastic world of the psychedelic drug.

(2) Another argument is that laws should be only about situations in which people hurt each other. A group of young people in a pad having a pot party claim that they are hurting nobody, and they believe the law is oppressive at this point and an invasion of privacy. They would say that if a drug is a menace to society that is one matter; but if it can be enjoyed innocently without being a threat to society, there should be no law against it.

105

(3) It is claimed that many young people have a deep religious need but that present forms of religion or present church life fails to satisfy it. Some of the great mystical experiences of the human race sound blasphemous when couched in Christian terms but this is very unjust. By the right use of psychedelic drugs many young people can be opened up to genuine spiritual experiences. Once such experiences are had by drugs they can then be had without drugs because an original breakthrough has been made.

(4) Young people with various kinds of emotional problems and cultural conflicts find that drugs help them work through to a solution to their problems. This does not mean that they are drugged into unreality. They may even go through some hours of psychological hell. But the problems are faced not dodged; they are fought not evaded; and a better person emerges from the experience.

(5) There is some evidence that alcoholism can be fought with psychedelic drugs. Who knows what other deep psychological problems can be aided this way? Or who knows what cases heretofore so very stubborn can be greatly helped by psychedelic drugs? And why is there not a possibility of a quick cure of many ordinary cases making unnecessary the many expensive visits to the psychiatrist?

There are Christian replies to such reasoning:

(1) All drugs that are addictive, such as heroin, and that are physiologically damaging (e.g., speed) are not drugs any Christian should have any traffic with.

(2) Prudence should certainly be the guide of the Christian in any cases of doubt. As long as there is no clearance of a drug by regularly constituted medical or drug-control organizations, it is no drug for a Christian. At the present time there is a flood of literature attempting to show the relative innocency of marijuana. The Christian should settle for nothing less than a clear and definitive answer that is beyond any reasonable possibility of laboratory reversal as to the harmfulness or harmlessness of any drug.

(3) It has been known for years that there is no such thing as innocent gambling. Wherever gambling is permitted, all sorts of secondary criminality is to be found. The same is true of drugs. The issue is not just the drug. The issue is what a host of evils always go with the usage of drugs. This is one of the fundamental reasons why most Christian ethicists are unimpressed by the so-called altruistic, psychologically remedial, or religious value of drugs.

(4) Drugs cost money. The more diligent the policing of the sale of drugs, the more the drugs cost. The teenager who wants to keep his addiction secret from his parents begins a career of lying, cheating, and petty thievery. Others participate in public begging such as has not been seen in America since the Great Depression.

As the cost of the habit increases, ways of getting money must become more criminal. The drug user must resort to grand theft or burglary. This is tough and mean business. In some states burglary calls for a mandatory five year sentence in a penitentiary. The judge can make no allowances. This is virtually condemning the young person to a life of crime.

(5) The purity of the drugs cannot be controlled. The purchaser is at the mercy of the seller—the dosage can be too strong, too weak, or cut with the wrong stuff. And therefore who can predict what the trip is going to be like? In a recent case the peddler was cutting his drugs with fatal doses of arsenic.

(6) There is always the danger of the drug user mixing drugs. Here again we run into the problem of potentializing a drug, that is, increasing its power a great deal. What is an ordinary amount of a drug becomes a catastrophic amount if taken with something else, for its effect can be greatly compounded.

The Christian ethicist must then register a strong veto against the use of drugs except in those instances where responsible medical people may use them on patients in a controlled situation. When some benefit is gained by treating a neurotic or psychotic condition, a drug may have some merit.

The really nagging question has not yet been answered. In schools lectures are given on drugs yet the students take drugs on the way to the lecture and some are under the influence of drugs while hearing of the evils of drugs.

Psychological studies are now in process attempting to get at the basic motivation for drug use. Some of these reasons have already been discussed. Perhaps there are many other causes at work which sociologists and psychologists will eventually unearth. But at least one factor seems obvious at this point. *We have an empty culture in which our teenagers and college students live.*

The chief complaint of high-school students about instruction in the use of drugs is that nothing is really said about what takes its place. It is true that some of the educational materials are hopelessly dated, but that is a technical problem which can be remedied. The question asked is: *if drugs are out, what is in?* Here the lecture suddenly goes flat. At the present young people will not give up drugs simply because they are told that drugs are harmful. They will perhaps even admit that a trip can be harmful. But in a life that is a vacuum, a bore, free from any significant challenge, what replaces the drug? Until that question is answered the "health courses" on drug abuse will be ineffectual.

Drugs fill up the vacuum of an empty culture. For example, work is a very therapeutic activity. But what work is left today for a teenager? Scientific gadgets within the house and professional care of the yard leave *nothing* for a young person to do. The millennial-long concept of established chores for young people is gone.

Sports have been another release for young people. But today even at the high-school level there is a professional spirit in sports. Only a very small fraction of a total student body actually participates in competitive sports. So as a major source of release for energies and emotions there is little to be had in sports except the routine gym classes.

Idealism in its many versions has been driven out of our school systems. Religion has been a great source of idealism, putting meaning and fiber in the life of a young person. Our "neutral" and "nonreligious" school systems have created an enormous vacuum at this point. Moral idealism is another source of inspiration and meaning for life, but little of this is taught any more even though it is supposedly official policy for the school system. Patriotism is also eroded in a number of ways. Many professors of political science think that the introduction to the subject must be the debunking of the constitution. This may be done by showing the historic origin of its various articles thus relativizing them, or by showing how a document written in the eighteenth century is obsolete in the twentieth century. Genuine criticism and historical assessment become either muck-raking or debunking. The traditional means of instilling some sense of idealism and purpose in the lives of students no longer exist. The evils of Puritanism is an endless theme, but the virtues of Puritanism are rarely mentioned. In many ways Puritanism was a powerful stimulus for good, but now it is a synonym for an ethical system with false values that produces false guilt and, therefore, psychologically damages children.

If an educational system is emptied of all forms of idealism and meaning, and substitutes teaching that is amoral and neutral toward important matters of idealism, and has no enduring set of values, then it is no surprise that drugs move in to fill the vacancy.

The Christian believes that anything that seriously harms the body is wrong. His stance concerning drugs is therefore basically a negative one. He may see that lectures on the evils of drugs are of some worth but by and large are ineffectual. Something has to be suggested to replace the drug. The Christian conviction is that the Christian way of life has those ingredients which make life meaningful and therefore undermine the psychological need for drugs.

Section 308: Homosexuality, Lesbianism

When men have sexual relationships with each other it is called homosexuality. When women have sexual relationships with each other it is called lesbianism (from the Greek town, Lesbo, where it was practiced by the priestess Sappho). People who have sexual relationships with those of the opposite sex are called heterosexual. *Time* of October 31, 1969, contains an extensive essay on homosexuality in America. Male homosexuality is reported to run as high as 10 percent of the male population. Lesbianism reportedly involves 4 percent of the female population with 2 percent being exclusively homosexual.

There are many forms of sexual perversion (described in the classic pre-Freudian work of Krafft-Ebing, *Psychopathia Sexualis*), but we are limiting our discussion to homosexuality (which will be understood to include lesbianism).

The issues about homosexuality are very complex and are not understood by most members of the Christian church. To them it is a vile form of sexual perversion condemned in both the Old and New Testaments (cf. Rom. 1:26–28).

A recognition of the different kinds of homosexuality must be the beginning of an intelligent discussion of the subject:

(1) Children experiment with each other sexually, but this kind of homosexuality normally disappears as the child matures.

(2) Men and women have homosexual relations when confined exclusively to the company of their own sex as in armies and penitentiaries. This is, however, "situational homosexuality" and again usually ends when the person returns to normal social relationships.

(3) Homosexual practices may be part of religious rites or done for the sake of pure sexual titillation. These forms of homosexuality were widely practiced in the ancient world and the biblical condemnations of homosexuality are usually addressed to these versions. Homosexuality as purely sexual titillation was a common Roman vice.

(4) Homosexuality is usually the product of a certain kind of destructive relationship within a family. The relationship of the mother and father can be such that it drives the child into homosexuality. Homosexual symptoms start before the third year. It is therefore a very deep-seated psychological problem.

The problem within the average Christian church is that almost all Christians believe that homosexuality is a perverse manifestation of sin and should be so treated. They are completely dense to the psychological factors which have produced the homosexual person. The one relief at this point is the famous Wolfenden Report made by the Church of England in 1957.

As far as Christian ethics is concerned, one fundamental distinction must be made: if the homosexual is a genuinely psychologically disturbed person that is one thing. The very fact that less than 5 percent of homosexuals are cured through psychotherapy indicates what a deep psychological problem it is. If a person is homosexual for purely sexual stimulation with no psychological pathology attached to it, that is another issue. There is enough popular and technical information on the subject so that no pastor need be ignorant of the facts of homosexuality as they have been scientifically ascertained.

Homosexuality takes on certain life patterns. There is the homosexual who is extrovertive and aggressive in his behavior. There is the homosexual who leads a secret, furtive, desperate life. There is the homosexual who marries to conceal his homosexuality. There is the person who is a sexual experimentalist and engages in homosexuality for the different sexual titillation it gives him. There is the "AC-DC" person—the person who is happy with heterosexual or homosexual experiences.

Some have believed that homosexuality is a physiological disease and not a psychological one. However, Frank Lake (*Clinical Theology*, chap. 10) claims that after the most exhaustive tests no physiological basis for homosexuality can be found. The notion that masculine looking women and effeminate men are homosexual is a popular myth and is not grounded in fact.

The church finds itself between a rock and a hard place. Psychiatrists have a clear picture of the kinds of homes or situations which tend to produce homosexuality. And although there are differing opinions at some points, psychiatrists generally recognize homosexuality as a psychological pathology. Therefore the church is dealing with a sick person and ought to be as redemptive and charitable as it can be. All of us go through this life only once and therefore the Christian church is committed to the redemptive attitude towards all of life.

Unfortunately there are some very unhappy features of homosexuality. Some homosexuals are crude and impulsive in their search for a partner. Others marry to conceal their homosexuality. Many engage in elaborate rationalizations to prove that homosexuality is one of the normal expressions of sexuality. Others attempt to show how much more creative the homosexual person is in contrast to the heterosexual person.

Two things must be understood by every pastor and church even if the homosexual person himself does not understand them: (1) Sexuality in the total range of living things is for reproduction. Some traces of homosexuality can be found among animals but this is sheer confusion on the part of the animals. Sexuality normally functions in the cycle of reproduction and therefore homosexuality can never compete as an alternate view of sexuality. (2) Parents whose own psychological patterns are normal uniformly produce heterosexual children. Homosexuality has to be the product of a home situation that is seriously psychologically pathological.

The problem facing a given local church is that it must be a church of *all* forgiven sinners and not just a church of *good* sinners which excludes *bad* sinners. It is also a church that seeks not only life everlasting but a meaningful life on this earth. It must find the way then of treating the homosexual as a genuinely forgiven person if he trusts in Christ; as a fellowship of the redeemed the church should help the homosexual find real meaning for his life; and at the same time the church must prevent the homosexual from letting his pathology get out of control and become the source of a serious difficulty in the church. There should be a frank confrontation with the homosexual in which the pastor (or whomever the church may appoint) confronts the homosexual with the fact that his pathology is understood and that he is not to be treated judgmentally but in grace, forgiveness, and redemption; and in return the homosexual must strive to be the essence of respectability in his conduct in the church.

Section 309: Transplants

The Jews, the Christians, and the Moslems have had strict ethical rules for many centuries before modern medicine about the mutilation of the body. Modern medicine has been slowly encroaching into the area of bodily mutilation—both in the adding of parts to the body (false teeth!) and in the use of metallic parts, especially in bone surgery, without any significant opposition. Organ transplantation has dramatically revived the historic ethical issues of most religious faiths on the mutilation of the body. For the most part the Christian church has found itself ethically unprepared for these kinds of developments.

In organ transplantation it is difficult to determine what is an ethical problem and what is a medical problem. Of one thing we can be sure —there is going to be continued expansion in the use of all sorts of organ implantations and in the use of machines to replace body organs. An enormous amount of research has already been done in the development of a mechanical heart. However, more detailed knowledge of the DNA molecules may enable doctors to regenerate diseased organs rather than transplant them.

Because the more dramatic kinds of transplants have received such world-wide attention, and because they are yet in such an experimental stage, it is very difficult to form any real Christian ethic about transplants at this time. We shall therefore discuss some of the matters which Christians think are at least potential ethical problems:

(1) *The problem of identity.* Does the implantation of an organ from one person to the body of another create an identity crisis in the person who has the transplant? The answer is that in some cases it causes an acute problem of identity. There is not only tissue rejection but "psychological" rejection. Some patients feel a sense of strangeness living by virtue of an organ from some other person. This is basically a psychological problem and indicates that some psychotherapy must go with major organ transplants if an identity crisis is to be avoided in the patient.

(2) *The problem of mutilation.* There is a long history of the ethical problem of mutilation among Christian theologians. The basic idea

(Jewish and Christian) is that the concept of the resurrection implies that the Christian suffer as little mutilation of the body in this life as possible. Organ transplanting seems to be a violation of the ethics of non-mutilation.

There is one simple refutation of this which makes the problem of no consequence for Christians. Because of the enormous populations of the Asiatic nations, cremation is the only realistic way to dispose of the dead. Bodily mutilation is no issue at all when contrasted with cremation. The fear of mutilation is purely a Western phenomenon that would cause chaos if introduced as an ethical principle in those Asiatic societies where cremation is mandatory.

(3) *The problem of defining death.* The issue of death and organ transplanting is this: if the person is really dead, then the organ is dead and a transplant is worthless; if the organ is alive, the person is alive and to remove one of his organs, especially the heart, is to medically murder the man.

Paul Ramsey has written a perceptive article, "On Updating Death" (*Religious Situation 1969,* chap. 15). He says that Senator Kennedy died three times. (i) When the bullet entered his brain at the moment of the firing of the gun, he was *practically* dead for nothing could reverse the damage. (ii) He was *medically* dead at 6:30 P.M., eighteen hours after the shooting when the brain waves did not register. (iii) He was *officially* dead the following morning at 1:44 A.M. when all the physiological processes of the body stopped. It can be added that apart from extreme cases where the body is destroyed almost all at once as in an intense fire or explosion, the different systems of the body die at different rates.

Transplantation of organs then takes place as the body is moving from one state of death to another. Ramsey's point is that we ought to have new medical definitions of death so that transplants could occur within a certain definition of death. Then any charges of murdering a patient for the sake of a transplant could be ruled out. As odd as it may seem, even with our present medical knowledge some counties or cities in our nation have not as yet formalized any theory of death.

(4) *The experimental state of medicine.* It is argued that transplants are immoral in that doctors do not know enough as yet to perform such surgery. Two replies may be made to this. Any sort of radical advance in science, which includes medicine, has to start when the

experimental data is not yet complete or the progress of science would be immeasurably slowed down.

There are many other kinds of experiments going on in the practice of medicine besides transplants but they do not make headlines. In such practices there is an outside chance that the cure for some disease or malady, which is up to this point incurable, will be found. Although transplants have a dramatic character to them they are not out of step with the kinds of things doctors and physiologists must do to keep the edge of medical science growing. And the general public is the benefactor of these advances from the growing edge of medicine.

(5) *The problem of consent.* The problem of consent is either a legal or a purely technical problem. The person with the organ for a transplant is usually in no condition to give consent for the removal of the organ. Who then gives the consent? There is also the factor of time. If the problem of consent becomes too technical or involved, the vital time range within which doctors must work is lost. This is a technical problem that will eventually be solved as the matter of transplanting becomes more frequent.

(6) *The problem of machines.* Can engineers working with doctors perfect machines so that transplants are not necessary? Perhaps given enough time this can be accomplished. For example, the number of good hearts available for replacement of bad ones is far too small. Only a small fraction of people who need new hearts can get them. The heart machine is the only real answer. But the chemical function of a liver or a kidney is so complicated that as yet nothing small enough to insert in a human body is anywhere within experimental consideration.

(7) *The problem of equity.* The number of life-saving machines (e.g., for kidneys) and the organs available for transplants is very limited. Who gets the use of the machine? who gets the new heart? This is a very difficult problem at the present and can be solved only by medical consultation of a staff of medical personnel. For example, should an important member of a community have precedence over John Doe? Sometimes when an organ is transplanted it is relatively so strong compared to the aged state of the other organs that it breaks them down. This also complicates the decision as to who the recipient should be.

Joseph Fletcher in his typical pioneering spirit says that rather than dragging on with medical and ethical analyses, transplanting should be set up as part of the regular hospital system. In this way thousands of people who now die from defective organs could be saved ("Our Shameful Waste of Human Tissue: An Ethical Problem for the Living and the Dead," *Religious Situation 1969,* chap. 14).

Somewhat the opposite of Fletcher's views are those of the Jehovah's Witnesses. Blood transfusions in particular seem offensive to them. An analysis of their position on this matter with their solution to the problem will be found in their journal, *Awake* (August 22, 1969).

(8) *The problem of meaning.* Medical experimentation along with most other experimentation is usually conducted on pragmatic and technical motivation. In medicine it is very frequently conducted on humanitarian grounds. Our Western culture is at present without a common religion, a common philosophy, or a common ethic. Yet much of what is done in medicine really presupposes some kind of belief beyond the technicalities of science. Why should a person's life be extended? Why should the ordinary course of the wasting away of tissue be halted? At present the only answers are technical or pragmatic or based on family sentimentality. But eventually we must come to an understanding of the human person that will in turn become the basis of an ethic that will guide medicine as much as it guides man's social and personal life. Until such a synthesis is reached organ transplanting exists in an ethical no man's land.

Section 310: Sexual Permissiveness

Modern books, plays, movies, magazines, court decisions, and radical changes in attitudes toward sexuality are all obvious witnesses to the fact that Western society has entered a phase of sexual permissiveness. Today what is commonplace in matters of sexual morality and pornography would have been persecuted to the full extent of the law with the almost universal approval of an indignant society not too many years ago.

Again we face a common problem. When we are in the midst of an obvious revolution, we find it the most difficult to know what the *real* causes are. Some of the reasons given are:

(1) The church has declined in membership (in terms of percentage of the total population) and prestige so that the moral force it used to exercise on society has been reduced to the minimum.

115

(2) Psychiatry since Freud has indicated the dangers to the self when matters are repressed or suppressed. We are now intentionally getting sexual matters out into the open for discussion so that they will not be psychologically damaging.

(3) The Puritan ethic is a guilt-producing ethic regarding sex, and to have happy sexual relationships we must abandon the kind of ethic that makes sexual experiences the causes of guilt and not of pleasure and companionship.

(4) The pattern of marriage in America has become sick. The new sexual permissiveness, misguided as it might prove to be from a later perspective, is but an effort to find a new pattern of sexuality and married life. The divorce rate, double standards, swinging parties, the call-girl racket, sexual hypocrisy among the elders—all are symptomatic to the younger set that traditional sexual mores have collapsed.

(5) The older pattern of an established home in an established community with an established family and an established job is being destroyed in huge cities where people are highly mobile. Mobility in megalopolis tends to create sexual permissiveness.

(6) Possible atomic war has shortened all our visions. One sociologist has figured out a formula of war-inflation and has come to the conclusion that the big bomb will go off in the year 2000 A.D. But young people think of life spans between five and ten years and not forty or fifty years. This makes for a *now* generation which makes for a *now* sex generation.

(7) Big cities cut off too many of the traditional out-of-doors activities of young people. Asphalt streets and miles of buildings drive young people into their pads with their records, their tape recorders, their dope, and their sex.

These are the more remote causes that are very hard to evaluate. It is difficult to point the finger at two items and state that they have caused the new sexual permissiveness.

However there are more immediate factors which at least facilitate the new permissiveness.

(1) Birth control pills eliminate the nuisance factor in all the older methods of birth control.

(2) The technological society which demands more and more years of education keeps postponing marriage. Modern young people are physiologically and emotionally ready for sexual experiences long before they finish their extended technological training.

(3) The divorce rate that has increased so greatly in the past two decades means that there is a large part of our population between marriages but not between sexual experiences.

(4) The knowledge explosion has had its influence on sexual permissiveness. Movies, television programs, millions of paperbacks, and unusually frank information in typical monthly women's journals have gone a long way toward educating people in sexual matters. What was once learned very poorly from parents or too sensationally from friends may now be learned from competent people through magazines, paperbacks, and television. The result has been the general freeing-up of large parts of our population about human sexuality in all its phases.

(5) Certainly one of the strongest forces in creating a new sexual permissiveness is the belief that the function of sex as pleasure can and ought to be separated from the function of sex for reproduction. This presumes of course the use of the pill. This idea is not intended to promote promiscuity. It simply means that when two people have very deep feelings for each other with a mutual respect for each other, sexual relationships are a proper means of a more fulfilling realization of the relationship. If a couple is mature in judgment, and mature in their emotions, then there is no real reason why they cannot have sexual relationships apart from marriage.

If a couple wish to make a permanent arrangement in marriage that is a good thing too. There is nothing prejudicial against marriage; there is only a prejudice against a society that thinks sexual experiences are to be had only in marriage.

Those who advocate the new permissiveness have certain reasons such as:

(1) If young people can see that sexual intercourse is not just for marriage and/or just for the procreation of children, but part of the natural joy and pleasure of life, then sexual experiences will cease to be damaging experiences. When sex is made so serious, treated as if it were dynamite, and surrounded with many irrational taboos, it becomes very damaging. Many marriages are either ruined or unhappy because the partners were hung-up on such a serious, morbid, moralistic view of sex. The present generation feels that one of the chief benefits of the new permissiveness is that it removes from sexual relationships all of these damaging attitudes.

(2) In expansion of the first point it can be said that an unusual

117

amount of guilt feelings gather around sexual intercourse, more perhaps than surround any other activity in which people participate. If sex can be seen as play, as pleasure, as natural, and as free from taboos, most of its power to produce guilt is removed. Nobody can make any insurances that sex can always be free from guilt feelings. But it is claimed that society would be much healthier if a lot of these guilt feelings could be eliminated or moderated.

(3) All forms of petting and necking and fondling are essentially frustrating. Sex play is preliminary to the sex act and to have the play without the act is to experience frustration. The new permissiveness would eliminate this kind of frustration.

(4) Sexual experiences before marriage are ways of "troubleshooting" marriages. How many bad marriages ending in divorce the new permissiveness would prevent cannot be calculated. But it is an assumption that people with some sexual experience are going to make better choices of mates than people without such experiences.

Of course, the new permissiveness not only presumes the almost universal use of the pill but the reconstruction of the law. The law as it now stands has rules that punish all sorts of sexual activities that are now being widely practiced and which are very private affairs. Proponents of the new permissiveness maintain that laws should not be written that pertain to what consenting adults may do in privacy. Laws should be concerned with practices, including sexual ones, which hurt, harm, or damage society or innocent or immature people.

The case for the new permissiveness is not quite as substantial as it has been made out to be:

(1) The new permissiveness is not totally dependent upon the pill but largely so. The pill has not received complete medical clearance. Neither is it one hundred percent effective in preventing pregnancies. In some cases it just doesn't work or the girls taking it do not faithfully follow the directions. So unwanted pregnancies may still occur with all the problems such pregnancies bring.

Further some serious side effects of the pill are beginning to show up making it yet a risk to a certain number of women. Whether more bad side effects will emerge or whether the present ones will be eliminated can only be known by much more experience with the pill.

(2) Venereal disease is on the increase. Regardless of the means that now exist to control it, venereal disease is not being controlled. Apparently women who take the pill will not take penicillin, or men

will not take the curative medicines. This is no innocent matter, no mere technicality, for at the present manner in which the new permissiveness is practiced venereal disease is a major health hazard.

(3) Regardless of what is said about sex being fun, play, and pleasure and not the serious matter formerly considered, this is just not the case. Powerful emotions still accompany sexual activity. Everybody has some hostility, some guilt, some feelings of inadequacy, some anxiety, and some areas of low tolerance. Sexual experiences can excite or disturb these emotions which cannot be turned on and off like an electric light switch. Therefore the potential damage of wrong sexual relationships is still present. In fact some of the most recent experiments show that frigidity among women is increasing especially in those girls who have had free sexual experiences before marriage. Somthing happens to these girls which psychiatrists are not yet sure of that makes them become frigid when they get married. It should be the reverse. The girl experienced in intercourse should make the better wife. But evidently there are psychological forces at work when teenage girls have premarital intercourse that creates frigidity in them when they marry. Of course this is not an assertion that this is *always* the case, but it is statement about percentages. The percentage of frigidity is rising in the married women who were sexually experienced many years before marriage.

(4) The new permissiveness seems to confuse sex with sexuality. By sex we mean the more immediate feelings and more physiological aspects of sexual relations. By sexuality we mean the total male-female relationship. Real healthy sex experience should always be within the context of sexuality. When sex is divorced from sexuality it becomes distorted. Or to put it another way, sex is an experience; sexuality is a total way of life. The real experience of sex must then always be within the total experience of sexuality. And to date there is no better solution for the population at large for creating the right relationships of sexuality than marriage.

There is no denying that ignorance about the physiology of sex and the psychology of sex and the technique of sex can make for trouble. Couples may need counseling and coaching at this level for marriages can be wrecked here too. But with the proper guidance many of these problems can be solved and then sexuality as something deeper and richer and more rewarding than sex can develop.

(5) The new permissiveness in sexual matters has one thing in re-

verse. It presumes that thrilling sexual experiences are the bases of real companionship. Satisfaction in sex is thus the foundation of harmony in life. Psychologically it is the reverse. A simple illustration will bring this contradiction to the surface. A couple has a long, bitter dispute in the evening over some financial matter. The wife feels that the most immediate need of the house is new drapes as they dress up the whole house. The man feels that the patio has to be enlarged for the benefit of the children to facilitate their playing. Will that couple go to bed with bitter experiences and have a happy sex experience? Hardly so! If, on the other hand, they have had a wonderful evening of eating at a good restaurant and seeing a very enjoyable movie, they will return home in the best of moods for a satisfactory sexual relationship. Happy sexuality has prepared the way for happy sex, and it doesn't work in reverse. There are certainly thousands of marriages every year that end up in the divorce court because the couple has the relationship of sex and sexuality in the reverse order.

Or to put it another way, sex must exist in the context of sexuality which means a significant relationship of the sexes before sexual intercourse; and it intends a meaningful relationship after intercourse. If intercourse is a mere event, a mere happening, it is bound to be superficial and frustrating. Sexuality presupposes a set of real relationships before intercourse and a life of mutuality after intercourse. In this context there is fulfillment in sex. But when there is sex with no sexuality then sex becomes episodic and superficial.

It has been said that the older a couple becomes the higher sex becomes. This is an odd sounding statement. It means that the longer people live together in harmony and mutuality, the more they mean to each other. Sex becomes less and less a factor and sexuality more and more a factor. A great backlog of common experiences, years of deepening experiences, and larger areas of mutuality all contribute to a richer man-woman relationship. Thus sex becomes less physiological and more spiritual, less episodic and more a way of life; there is less emphasis on pleasure and more on satisfying and rewarding experiences.

The most frequent criticism of the Playboy version of sex is that it is sex in isolation. The girl is a physically attractive creature from nowhere; the man is some virile specimen of masculinity from nowhere. The act of intercourse is between two people who come from nowhere and go nowhere. This is sex at its most superficial and unrealistic manifestation.

For a general critique of the Playboy philosophy of sex see B. R. Walker's *The New Immorality*—unexpectedly written by a Unitarian. He accuses Hefner of continually promising to produce the complete Playboy philosophy of sex. He adds that to date Hefner has not been able to do this.

(6) A secondary element in the new permissiveness in sex is the belief that interracial sexual relationships should be considered as normal and as free from prejudice as marriages within a racial group. Any two people who are emotionally mature should be free to have sexual relations and feel free to marry. Two black psychiatrists wrote a book, *Black Rage*, that challenges this assumption.

In a happy sexual relationship the experience is satisfactory only if the conditions are psychologically healthy. Part of this psychological element is the way in which a person thinks of himself as a sexual partner, and part is how he thinks of his relationship to his partner. *Black Rage* indicates that sexual relationships between blacks and whites are generally poor for psychological reasons. Neither partner sees himself in his right sexual role and as a result the relationship is a poor or frustrating one. For example, it is very difficult for the black girl to feel herself a real, qualified sexual mate. She finds it almost impossible to get over the idea that the white partner is exploiting her. What may be ethically or morally defended runs aground on unexpected psychological factors.

There is no question that the Western world is trying to find a new pattern of sex and sexuality. At the present time we can say that all the wrongs attributed to the so-called Puritan ethics are not as wrong as usually represented. The Puritan ethic retains many of the essential ingredients of a happy sexual relationship. And there is no mountain of evidence to prove that the new permissiveness has created a sexual Utopia among those who practice it. Many of the traditional problems (which are usually attributed to the ethics of the Puritans) of sexual relationships persist and reappear in the new permissiveness. The new permissiveness is not pure gain with no losses.

There is currently a debate that only time can settle. It has been presumed that pornography, nudity in all sorts of media and entertainment, and so-called "girlie films" excite men sexually and increase the rate of sexual crimes. Reports from the Scandinavian countries that have taken the restrictions off such matters and the almost abandonment of pornographic censorship in America at the present time give evidence of reducing the number of sexual crimes. The theory is that these kinds of open and free exposure of sex and sexual themes become substitutes for sexual experiences or releases of sexual tensions. Whether this represents a permanent factor in society for reducing sexual crimes or a low dip of a curve that is suddenly going to zoom upward must be left to time to tell. The president of the United States rejected the findings of a presidential committee on sex and pornography in America. The problem awaiting resolution is whether this rejection was a shrewd political maneuver or whether the researchers were so prejudiced *before* their investigation that their investigation is more a recording of their opinion than the facts.

Section 311: Suicide

Most discussions of suicide in books on ethics or theology are useless. Where soldiers, spies, or virgins commit suicide to prevent a greater evil represent so small a number of people as not to merit discussion. Most of the suicides reported in the papers are committed by disturbed people who act compulsively and are therefore not ethical problems.

The only significant discussion of the topic that has an ethical relevance to it is to be found in Paul Tillich's *Systematic Theology*, II, 75–76. In this discussion Tillich admits indebtedness to Kierkegaard's *The Sickness unto Death*.

We might coin a term here: *mini-suicide*. The point is not that a person kills himself. He does not do that in the vast majority of *mini-suicide*. A *mini-suicide* is a retreat from life. It is facing a conflict and instead of attempting to resolve it, fleeing from it. To use one of Tillich's famous phrases it is a failure in "the courage to be."

There are thousands of versions of *mini-suicides*: retreat from conflict; failure to assume responsibility; shirking one's duty; passing the buck; becoming impassive before human need or suffering; surrendering to despair rather than grasping hope; avoidance of the personal relationship and retreating into the crowd or into loneliness; etc.

The ethical point here is that these people are still within the range of normal response where neurotic or psychotic suicides are not. These people are confronted with situations where they can and ought to respond the right way but they retreat. And this retreat is an unethical retreat and therefore wrong.

Herrmann Hesse's *Steppenwolf* (the lone wolf of the steppes, a novel that has exerted a great influence on hippie thought) already anticipated Tillich's idea of a *mini-suicide*. He speaks of the "little personality" who commits suicide in his retreat from life in contrast to the ordinary pathological suicide (cf. pp. 54–55).

V

THE WIDER IMPLICATIONS
OF CHRISTIAN ETHICS

Section 400: The Basis for a Wider Perspective

Christianity is the religion of redemption through faith in Jesus Christ. This salvation includes not only a conception of the church and the kingdom of God, but it also includes a conception of ethics. It recognizes that man has other needs than those which can be classified as "spiritual" and that these needs must also be ministered to. What evangelical Christianity resists is the effort to interpret Christianity as if it were *only* an ethical system. This is what the Deists attempted to do; this is what the great German philosopher, Kant, attempted to do; and this is what Braithwaite in modern times has attempted to do in his famous essay, "An Empiricist's View of the Nature of Religious Belief." This essay has been reprinted in many books. It may be found in I. T. Ramsey's *Christian Ethics and Contemporary Philosophy*, chapter 3.

The mission of the Christian church is to teach the Word of God, preach the gospel, and evangelize the non-Christian world. But it must not be deadened to the manifestation of love and justice toward people's needs which cannot be classified as "spiritual." The purpose of foreign missions is primarily the spread of the Christian gospel but this does not preclude the missionary from doing tasks in varied fields of endeavor such as agriculture, medicine, and education.

Personal faith in Christ is the end of the gospel. In spite of all the mean things said about this, it is not a piece of religious selfishness. It is not a sop for exploited people, an opiate for depressed populations, nor a religious narcotic enabling people to endure the misery of this world until they enjoy the glories of heaven.

124

Holy Scripture suggests that Christian man and the Christian church have a much larger range of responsibility than this. The following is the evidence for the wider responsibilities of the Christian:

(1) The biblical doctrine of creation makes man the lord of creation. This means that there must be a society within which man achieves this lordship and that Christian man's responsibilities have to do with creation as well as redemption. God created a humanity and a humanity is a society. The Christian man must endeavor to make that society conform to the will of God the best he can regardless of the presence of sin and evil in that society.

(2) Many of the ethical assertions of the Old Testament are social in nature. This does not mean that the church is to follow nor recreate the Old Testament ethic. But it does show that God's concerns with Israel were not purely spiritual, religious, and cultic but also social, economic, and political. To the Christian this means that God does have these concerns even if they are not repeated in so many words in the New Testament.

(3) A number of the outbursts of the Old Testament prophets were to point out that the religious or cultic life of Israel was an offense to God because social evils were tolerated or went unjudged. God has not changed his mind about social evil in the New Testament period.

(4) Matthew 22:15–22 is the famous passage on rendering unto God what belongs to God and rendering unto Caesar what belongs to Caesar. No doubt the church has read too much into this passage. But it does indicate Christian social responsibility in a general way.

(5) The parable of the Good Samaritan (Luke 10:29–37) was surely told to indicate that meticulous religious practice is no substitute for an act of specific mercy to a human being in desperate need.

(6) The account of the rich man and Lazarus (Luke 16:19–31) teaches that being merciless to the poor is contrary to the divine will.

(7) Our Lord made the remarkable statement that to feed the hungry, to give water to the thirsty, to give hospitality to the stranger, to clothe the naked, to visit the sick, and to visit the prisoners were acts which ministered to Christ himself (Matt. 25:31–46).

(8) Our Lord also said that Christians are light and salt for the world as seen *in their good works* (Matt. 5:3–16).

(9) The love of one's neighbor is the second Great Commandment (Matt. 22:39) and therefore love can only be fulfilled in its outreach to one's neighbor.

125

(10) Romans 13:1–7 sets forth the relationship of the Christian to the state. This is one of the most controversial passages in the New Testament. However it is interpreted, it does commit the Christian to *some* responsibility to the state and therefore to *something* Christian about the social order. The Christian and the Christian church cannot express their responsibility to God only in a spiritual way or inside the four walls of the church.

(11) 1 Peter 2:13–17 says that Christians are to be subject to every human institution (*ktisis*). This can only mean that the Christian has a responsibility to agencies within the government, structures within the government, or perhaps societies or organizations within society that are not necessarily government structures. However, Peter does give us an idea of what he has in mind by the concrete advice he gives: respect the emperor; respect governors; honor all men; love the brotherhood; fear God; and honor the emperor. These are social and not "spiritual" concerns.

(12) There is some version of natural law in Romans 2:12–16. By definition natural law is that which is binding on all men as God's creatures. However this difficult passage is interpreted, it does bind the Christian to some sort of natural law, and therefore he must have something in his ethics that is social in character.

(13) The Scripture treats man as a whole and not just as a spiritual being who worships God. All of man's life is included in the perspective of divine revelation. Therefore for *emphasis* we may stress the priority of man's spiritual concerns, but this emphasis must not blind the church from seeing the total man in his total need.

(14) The church is part of the kingdom of God. The kingdom of God is wider than the church. This much is expressed in Matthew 16:18–19. Therefore the larger concerns of the kingdom are also the concerns of the church. The kingdom of God includes in its perspective the whole sweep of history, the totality of the human race, and man in all his functions, secular as well as religious. In this sense the church must include some larger kingdom concerns in its ethics.

(15) Lutherans with their doctrine of the two kingdoms or the two rules of God, and Calvinists with their idea of common grace, and Anglicans with their specific idea of the relationship of church and state are all saying at least one thing in common: God is concerned with human civilization as well as the growth, spread, and health of the church.

Christian ethics must then have in its vision what we may provisionally call the total welfare of human civilization.

In his ethical theory, Kant has made famous the concept of a *categorical imperative*. He contrasts it with a hypothetical imperative. "If a man wants a strong heart, he must jog some every day" is a hypothetical imperative because a man may or may not want a heart in good shape. But an ethical statement is not optional. It is an imperative, an ought, a duty. So the expression "categorical imperative" indicates that a moral principle is not a matter of choice but contains a *must* and an *ought*. From the Christian standpoint Brunner rephrases Kant and writes a book on *The Divine Imperative*. In this work Brunner develops an ethic of three circles which parallels the previous discussion: (i) There are the orders of God for creation. These are ethical teachings for man as man, man as creature, man in creation, and man in society. (ii) Due to man's sin there must be added to this orders of sin, that is, ethical principles or rules that regulate man as sinner; and (iii) orders of redemption or those ethical principles that pertain to man as redeemed or man as in the Christian church.

This theory is similar to Abraham Kuyper's theory of spheres. Human culture is made up of spheres—economic, political, educational. Each of these spheres is autonomous, that is, it is ruled from within by the characteristics special to each sphere. Therefore any treatise on Christian ethics must adjust itself to the specific situations that obtain in each sphere.

We conclude this section then by asserting that the Christian church must include in its ethics something wider than the concerns of personal ethics or the immediate concerns of the ethical life of the church. The church must relate itself to the larger social, economic, educational, and political welfare of humanity.

But it must do this on a proportionate basis. It has neither the money nor the people to do all that it ought to do or wants to do or sees as its duty to do. It must therefore carefully study its priorities in order to do the best it can within its limitations of money and people.

Section 401: The Social Gospel

A movement known as the Christian Commonwealth Community published a magazine with the title, *The Social Gospel*. This is historically the first occurrence of the term. It became the expression used to designate in America during the late nineteenth and early twentieth century a movement in American churches which stressed the function of the church in society as a reforming social institution. Handy defines it as a movement of "liberally oriented, progressive-minded, moderately reformist current in social thought and action which became an effective force in a number of mainline Protestant denominations, especially in the North, in the early decades of the twentieth century," ("The Social Gospel in Historical Perspective," *Andover Newton Quarterly,* January, 1969).

This was a specific American way of stating the function of the church with reference to the larger concerns of society. It became "sloganized" and "codified" as the Social Gospel. Sometimes it was used in a vindictive way to show that the liberal Christian was concerned with all of man's needs whereas the evangelical Christian was caught in the web of a traditional form of Christianity in which the sole function of the church was to preach a gospel of personal salvation.

Of course social concern in the church was not born in the year 1900, the beginning of the "Christian Century." Ernst Troeltsch, *The Social Teachings of the Christian Churches* (the classic work on the subject in two volumes), G. W. Forell, editor, *Christian Social Teachings,* E. Westermarck, *Christianity and Morals,* T. C. Hall, *History of Ethics within Organized Christianity,* and E. L. Long, *A Survey of Christian Ethics* reveal Christian social ethics as part of the Christian faith and practice from the inception of the Christian church.

Of course the expressions "social ethics" or "Social Gospel" and "social action" are recent ones but the idea is old. For example, Luther had a social ethics built on three pillars: (1) The political use of the law was to guide governors of the state in matters of social justice. (2) God has two regiments whereby he fights the devil. He fights the devil in the church by the preaching of the Word of God; and he fights the devil in society through the state; and (3) each Christian expresses his social concern for his neighbor in fulfilling the commandment of loving his neighbor. G. W. Forell has given us a carefully documented summary of Luther's ethics in his work *Faith Active in Love.*

Calvin not only preached and taught in the city of Geneva, but he took an active part in the city's total life. For example, Calvin diagramed the sewer system for the city, codified its ordinances of civil law, and helped establish the weaving industry in the city. He did have a social ethics even though the term was not used in those days. The formalization of his views of the state form the last chapter of *The Institutes of the Christian Religion* (bk. IV, chap. 20). In the new translation of Calvin in *The Library of Christian Classics* (vol. 21, p. 1485), there is an extensive footnote citing materials about Calvin's view of the state and social ethics.

Great concern about the relationship of the Christian church and social problems was expressed in the nineteenth century in England, Germany, and America. The principle cause for this activity was the Industrial Revolution. Problems were created by the Industrial Revolution that the historic approaches to social ethics in the church were not adequate to resolve. It could be said that the Industrial Revolution created the Social Gospel (or whatever name it went under).

The usual formula of faith in Christ for personal salvation and love of neighbor for social problems was inadequate. Or the "render to God . . . render to Caesar" formula was too short for the problems faced. The theory of "change the heart and one changes society" was also a blanket that proved to be too short for the bed.

Clearly the church needed a new social ethics to come to terms with the Industrial Revolution. As a result a series of Christian social movements began in the nineteenth century to help the church grapple with these new problems. Many of these problems are with us today and still remain unsolved or only partially resolved. It was in this period that Christian Socialism came to prominence in Europe. This accounts for the fact that in their earlier days most of the neoorthodox and existential theologians were Christian Socialists. (F. D. Maurice, 1805–1872, an English theologian, was the first theologian to use the expression "Christian Socialism.") In America the reaction to the Industrial Revolution took the form of the Social Gospel.

There were other powers at work forcing the church to new thoughts about social ethics. Already we have mentioned the Deists and Kant who wished to reduce Christianity to only an ethical way of life. Kant's work, *Religion within the Limits of Reason Alone* (1793), exerted an enormous influence in interpreting religion as primarily ethics. Ritschl's (1822–1889) idea of the kingdom of God as a society of men ruled by the ethic of the love of Jesus was another powerful force at work in recasting the social ethics of the church.

The historic division of church and state, or church and world, was beginning to erode. The church was looked upon as God's agency to bring the kingdom of God into the world and to so Christianize civilization.

Walter Rauschenbusch (1861–1918) is looked upon as the theologian of the Social Gospel in America. But he was anticipated by such men as Channing, Bushnell, Parker, Colwell, Chapman, Gladden, Herron, Henderson, and Mathews. Rauschenbusch was awakened to the social issues of his times by his experiences as pastor of the Second German Baptist Church of New York. Raised in an individualistic, pietistic tradition he found this tradition helpless in coping with the massive ills he saw in New York City. Upton Sinclair's *The Jungle* is a famous book showing the effects among the laborers of the Industrial Revolution in the slaughter industry in Chicago. This situation in New York converted Rauschenbusch to the Social Gospel which he expressed in his two famous books, *Christianizing the Social Order* and *A Theology for the Social Gospel*. In *The Impact of American Religious Liberalism,* Kenneth Cauthen devotes an entire chapter to Rauschenbusch. He sets out the data in much more detail than we can give here.

Cauthen's book has another important element which we have not elaborated upon. He shows how the Social Gospel fitted into the total spectrum of liberal theology in America.

The term Social Gospel expressed two major ideas: (1) It repudiated evangelical Christianity because it was a religion concerned with one's personal salvation and not with man's total range of needs. Its motto "change the heart and you change society" was inadequate. The problems were too massive for such a simple solution. If this meant, for example, that there would be no change in safety rules for mines until the owner of the mine was converted, this would be a very cruel ethic as far as the miners were concerned. (2) It meant to say that God's concern for human redemption and salvation not only included the individual in his personal religion, but mankind in its institutions.

The kinds of changes Rauschenbusch himself was concerned with were: abolition of special privilege; unionization of labor; democratization of the economic order; and the formation of consumer cooperatives. Later on the Social Gospel added to its agenda racial justice, pacifism, and prohibition.

The fundamentalist considered the Social Gospel the betrayal of the gospel. The Social Gospel affirmed the brotherhood of man; fundamentalism taught the sinnerhood of man. The Social Gospel taught the fatherhood of God; fundamentalism taught that man became God's child only through faith in the unique sufferings of Christ. The Social Gospel made the distinction between the church and the world relative; fundamentalism saw the church as God's redeemed people and separate from the world. That God was at work in the world in many ways the fundamentalists would not deny. God was still Creator and Lord of the race. But to speak of a Social Gospel was to confuse the whole perspective of the work of God in the world. Furthermore many of the fundamentalists were premillennialists and believed God's kingdom could be set up only by God's King, Jesus Christ. The Social Gospel was to them the liberal version of postmillennialism whereby man through his own power and efforts would bring in the kingdom.

Some theologians saw a new Pelagianism in liberalism. The very idea that the church could "bring in the kingdom" apart from any special or supernatural help from God was to grossly underestimate the power of sin and attribute to man spiritual or moral powers which he does not have.

Liberalism was also accused of optimism unjustified by the character of human history. Its very intention of bringing in the "Christian Century" revealed a naïve optimism. And such optimism is also Pelagianism.

At the present time the issue is stalemated. The liberals have said that they did not underestimate sin and overestimate man's powers. And some claim to have been "chastened" by developments in the twentieth century, by the history of the century itself, and by neoorthodoxy. They call themselves "realists" meaning by the term frank, realistic appraisers of human sinfulness.

There is some discussion today as to whether the term Social Gospel is still a relevant expression. With the very recent social foment of thought and action in America, the liberal position expressed by the term "Social Gospel" is considered dated. The discontent with the expression is based on the belief that Christian social action rests on other presuppositions than those of the Social Gospel. The phrase "social action" has virtually replaced the expression "Social Gospel." Newer theories of Christian social ethics are being formed which are much more radical and different than the historic Social Gospel. In fact, in the new "theology of hope," *revolution* has become part of Christian social ethics which is a radical departure from the older Social Gospel (cf. W. Capps, editor, *The Future of Hope,* and Jürgen Moltmann's new book, *Religion, Revolution and the Future*).

Section 402: Universal Respect of Persons

America is a racially pluralistic society. Due to the historical factors which made the nation, it is inevitably a nation with a large white majority. The white people of America made the law; they made up the personnel of the police force; they administered the courts; and they ran the penal institutions. However, the events in America since the end of World War II have forced the white majority to recognize the racial pluralism in America and to start making amends so that all races can become equal partners in all aspects of American life.

The purpose of this section is not to offer solutions or programs for this problem. Among the black community there are a number of programs entertained which intend to give the black people just and fair treatment in every dimension of American culture. We cannot be the umpire with regard to these theories. There is also emerging a black theology (cf. the statement of the black theologians in *The Christian Century,* October 15, 1969). The issue in Christian ethics is to ascertain how racial and national groups should treat each other. Each country has its own pattern of internal conflicts of race against race or group against group. The question before the Christian is the analysis of this situation and the Christian attitudes toward the problems which the analysis brings to the surface.

(1) Regardless of color or race or national origin, groups of people throughout the world have disliked each other, have hated each other, and have persecuted each other. *The phenomenon is universal.* The reading of world history alone reveals the antagonisms of the centuries. The author has lived in Europe and the Middle East and traveled in the Orient and South America. Patterns of hatred, discrimination, persecution (which takes on so many disguised forms), and resentment are to be found everywhere.

In a given city where most of the city is of one race and one national allegiance, one part of the city may have a strong hatred for people who live in another part of the same city.

In a given nation with a common heritage of centuries of duration, there is usually one part of the nation which thinks it is superior to another part of that very same nation.

A group of nations usually forms a cultural area or a cultural belt. The same phenomenon appears here. One segment of this cultural belt will consider itself superior to the other parts of the same cultural belt.

In recent history Hitler's racial theory and the terrible practices that emerged from his ideas of racial superiority are well known. We have written a sad chapter in America because some whites have believed that racially they were superior to American blacks, American reds, and American chicanos. As aggravated as the problem may appear to some groups in America, it must be seen in light of the fact that this phenomenon is universal. It is not a peculiar American problem. We also have in America people who believe that those who have migrated from one part of Europe are superior to people who have migrated from another part of Europe. *Unfortunately ethnic, national, and racial conflict is a universal phenomenon.* It has existed in all centuries; it exists in all parts of the world.

(2) At the present time no proof is forthcoming that one racial or ethnic group is intellectually superior to any other.

That the peoples of the world differ in physical appearance and characteristics is an obvious fact. It is upon these differences that racial classifications are made. Although some anthropologists believe that the physical differences among people do not justify any racial classification, most anthropologists believe that the world is made up of three basic groups: the Caucasians (usually "the whites" but it does include the brown-skinned Indians of India); the Negroids (or the black people of the world which includes not only people in Africa but people of the Melanesian Islands); and the Mongoloids (Japanese, Chinese, American Indians, etc.). Some groups defy classification such as the white, hairy Ainu of Japan, the aborigines of Australia, and the pygmies.

Exhaustive tests have been made on the people of the world to determine the rate of the heart beat, rate of breathing, occurrence of blood types, etc. Any differences that emerge are insignificant in that they show no basis for racial superiority. Races or subracial groups that are big may have advantages in some of the sports (football, basketball); but on the other hand the Ping-Pong champions of the world

133

have been small people. Racial differences do exist, and they do give certain kinds of purely physical superiority, but when it comes to reason, mentality, etc., there is no racial superiority to be found. A recent anthropological study has claimed that centuries of a deficient diet have made a permanent genetic lowering of the intelligence quotient of blacks. At the time of this writing, however, the claim is still controversial among scientists.

When intelligence tests were first invented and used, it appeared as if certain races were superior to other races, or certain ethnic groups were superior to others. Upon further investigation it was found that such tests were valid only within a uniform cultural area. A person who is raised in one culture and takes a test in another culture scores very low. The low score does not indicate intellectual inferiority but cultural differences. For example, a person who migrated from Poland to America will score lower on an intelligence test in America when compared with established Americans.

Recently it has been shown that even in a given cultural area there are different levels in that cultural area itself which govern scores in intelligence tests. A student raised in a poor home with no magazines or books or perhaps even a radio does not score as high as the child who is raised in a middle-class home with lots of books and magazines in the house. Intelligence scores can be raised or lowered by changing a child's cultural backdrop. This has been proved by the study of identical twins who have been adopted into different homes.

Now there is evidence that racial communities in America represent different kinds of culture, and intelligence tests which ignore this factor are not valid.

This means that intelligence tests which seemed to indicate superiority of one group in a culture over another group must be reexamined in view of cultural differences within an area heretofore thought to be culturally uniform.

It is now generally believed that all so-called racial or ethnic superiority is really a cultural superiority. A person with a good mind raised in a poor culture scores poorly in intelligence tests. All supposedly technological degrees of civilization superiority are not racially determined but reflect cultural factors.

The most persistent mistake that laymen or uninformed people make is to presume that cultural differences are proofs of ethnic, national, or racial superiority. To put it bluntly, primitive peoples are primitive because they have primitive minds; superior civilizations are superior because the people who have created a superior civilization are superior people. This is wrong. These differences are cultural not racial.

Primitive cultures tend to be rigid cultures. They resist change. Any American can drive off the highway onto the dirt roads of Arizona and New Mexico and find Indians living in the Stone Age. This manifests what anthropologists already know, namely, that primitive cultures tend to be very rigid and fight change. This is why we still find Stone Age people in America. It might appear that these are inferior people who cannot live in an advanced society. To the contrary, it is the manifestation of cultural factors which are well known to anthropologists. The first and hardest lesson to learn in thinking about ethnic, national, and racial problems is that *cultural differences do not indicate racial differences*. Therefore cultural differences can never be the basis of drawing conclusions about racial superiority.

(3) The Christian ethic at this point must then be that any practice of any kind based upon a theory of racial, ethnic, or national superiority is wrong. Or to state it positively, every group of any kind (ethnic, racial, national) must treat every other group with equal respect *in all matters.*

The ethical evil in the idea of one group believing itself to be superior to another group is that the superior group believes that it is under a different set of ethical norms than the inferior group. *Ideas of racial superiority uniformly produce a double ethic: one for the superior group and one for the inferior group.*

The superior group feels that it has special rights and special privileges, and that it is due special treatment because it is the superior group. In addition to this the superior group feels that it is justified in treating the inferior group in a way that would be unethical if they treated each other in such a manner. They assume that it is not unethical to submit the inferior group to: limitations of all kinds, exploitations, discriminations, legal shortcuts, different standards in law enforcement, harsh and punitive penalties, brutal treatment, and even execution.

Modern examples of this that are too painful to sensitive Christian conscience are: Hitler's treatment of the Jews on the premise of Aryan racial superiority; the whites' treatment of the blacks in America based on a belief of white racial superiority; and the *apartheid* theory practiced in South Africa.

135

If all ethnic, national, and racial groups are equal, if there is no such thing as racial superiority, then no moral, ethical, political, economic, or educational policy can be put into practice which presumes racial superiority. There can be no justifiable double standard among peoples.

(4) Holy Scripture is in accord with what the physical anthropologists and psychologists teach about the unity of the human race, but Scripture uses theological language and concepts to express it.

Holy Scripture knows of only *one* humanity. Creation may have started with a pair but a whole humanity was intended. The name Adam can stand for a race as well as a man. Paul's great treatise on human sin (Rom. 1–3) is based on the presupposition that the human race is one humanity. The famous Adam-Christ chapters, Romans 5 and 1 Corinthians 15, presuppose one common humanity. Paul's statement of Acts 17:26 ("he made from one every nation of men") teaches us that there is only one humanity before God. In fact all statements in Scripture about the object of God's love, the scope of the cross, and of world-wide evangelism presume that there is but one humanity before God. Holy Scripture does mention peoples and nations of all sorts, but such distinctions are all relative and limited in contrast to the revelation and redemption of God intended for the entire human race.

The selection of the Jewish people for a unique role in world redemption (Rom. 9:1–5) is repeatedly declared in the Book of Deuteronomy as an election of grace, and is not based on any superiority of the Hebrew nation. The same truth is taught in Romans 9–11 where Paul affirms that Israel's special position in God's purposes is the result of an election of *grace* and if of grace then it is not based on any kind of superiority.

The most common appeal from Scripture to reenforce ideas of racial superiority *and with it a double ethic* is Genesis 9:20–28. It can be said in summary that the best exegesis of the passage today (Roman Catholic, Protestant, Jewish) supports no such interpretation. The older interpretation that Ham means "black" is no longer supported by the linguistic evidence. In fact there is no current knowledge of the derivation of the term. Using modern terms Noah was a Caucasian, and unless there was a miracle wrought by God a Caucasian husband and a Caucasian wife could not give birth to a Negroid child. Furthermore whatever the curse of Canaan was (note the shift in the narrative from Ham to Canaan), it was something fulfilled in that ancient world and has no application to modern man, modern races, and modern problems. The passage can be appealed to today only by using a false interpretation of its meaning to support a modern prejudice.

Holy Scripture knows of only one gospel for the whole world (Acts 4:12). There are not several gospels each adjusted to a different kind of humanity. All the race is sinful; all the race is guilty; all the race stands in need of God's mercy; and all the race needs salvation through faith in Christ.

From time to time in the exploration of the world explorers came across people who were so primitive that they did not believe these people had souls. Unfortunately such beliefs have been held in America. This is neither scientific nor biblical. When these "soulless" primitive peoples are given the same kind of education as people with souls they perform on the same high level. The aborigines of Australia were once held to be soulless creatures at the very bottom of the ladder called humanity. Yet when some of these people were educated, they became expert mathematicians. The "soulless" theory is non-Christian for Holy Scripture recognizes only one human race and each member of this race has, or in terms of more recent studies is, a soul. Any idea that such people can be treated in a brutal way because they do not have souls is based either on ignorance or prejudice. Whatever the justification, it is unchristian.

Holy Scripture knows only one church: "There is neither Jew nor Greek, there is neither slave nor free, there is neither male nor female; for you are all one in Christ Jesus," (Gal. 3:27–28 RSV). The same truth is taught in Acts 2 where the Holy Spirit is promised to *all flesh,* that is, regardless of any of the distinctions that human beings may make.

What is true of the oneness of man in redemption is based on the unity of man in creation. The belief of racial superiority with its inevitable double ethic is unknown to Holy Scripture.

This does not mean that there must be cultural uniformity. Any group of people within a state may wish to perpetuate many elements of its original culture. It has a right to its subculture within the context of a larger national culture. Democracy does not mean the end of individuality of persons or groups.

The Christian ethic of justice is that the rules of the game should be the same for all peoples. From the Christian standpoint basic equality must exist in all the basic structures of the state such as its economic system, its political system, its policing system, and its penal system.

The Christian is also a realist. He knows that prejudices and inequalities are going to continue to exist. He knows that feelings and prejudices built up over the centuries cannot vanish overnight with the passing of a law. Injustice, restrictions, discriminations, and unjust penalties are here to stay for some time. But it is the obligation of the Christian to point out that man does fall short not only of the glory of God but of the justice, equity, and love of God. He wants to witness to the inherent evil in any system that perpetuates a double standard of treatment among its citizens. He wills to unmask the specious arguments that support unequal practices and unjust discriminations. In a word, he wants equal respect for all persons in all the basic structures of a city, a county, a state, and a nation.

Section 403: Selective Pacifism

War has been a way of life for man since his first empires were founded thousands of years before Christ. The history of pacificism has been much more uneven. Only in the past few centuries has theory about the evil of war become very articulate. Our purpose is not to discuss the various theories of pacifism at this point. There is much existing literature on this subject. Our concern is the one raised by the Nuremberg trials and the attempt to apply its rules to current and future wars.

Does the individual have the right to decide if a war is just or not and have his decision honored by the government?

Does the individual have the right to decide if warfare of a particular kind is wrong or immoral and refuse to follow a certain policy or use a special weapon?

The Nuremberg trials seemed to defend the thesis that the individual citizen has the right to choose his wars and the right to disobey orders which he thinks are wrong.

Article 6 of the Nuremberg trials lists three kinds of war crimes: (1) Crimes against peace which mean it is a crime to plot war; (2) crimes that are contrary to the humanitarian manner in which war is to be fought; (3) very cruel kinds of crimes against humanity such as murder, extermination, enslavement, and deportation.

Article 8 reads: "The fact that the Defendant acted pursuant to the order of the Government or of a superior shall not free him from responsibility, but may be considered in mitigation of punishment if the Tribunal determines that justice so require."

There are three differing interpretations of these articles:

(1) The trials were out of order. War is war and there is no justification for trying the losing side as war criminals. If the situation were reversed and the allies had lost, the peoples of the allied nations would have considered it a great injustice if their leaders were tried and executed or jailed. The trials were more a form of disguised punishment than real cases of law. Therefore at the present time no draftee can appeal to the Nuremberg trials, nor may any American soldier make an objection to policies or weapons, based upon the articles of the Nuremberg trials.

(2) The trials were concerned with excessive crimes. They apply only to the most aggravated cases possible. Therefore no American has the right to protest the Viet Nam War on the basis of the Nuremberg trials because the United States Army is not perpetrating the brutal inhumanities of the Nazis in World War II.

(3) The Nuremberg trials set an international precedent. Every citizen has the right to decide if a war waged by his country is just or not. He has the right to decline to fight if he thinks the war is unjust. "My country right or wrong" is a slogan the Nuremberg trials made obsolete.

The trials also made it the responsibility of the civilian or soldier to decide if a given policy or weapon is inhuman. Bombs that shred things and people into little bits, germ warfare, chemical warfare, or the use of napalm are the kinds of weapons a soldier could object to as a matter of conscience.

At the present time American soldiers may not appeal to the Nuremberg trials regarding the manner in which the war is being fought in Viet Nam. But it cannot be denied that something is happening to the American people. This is the first war reported by television. With satellites, direct pictures of the war in Viet Nam may be seen by television. Further, our newspapers and national magazines are giving the American people news reporting in a depth heretofore not possible. The result is a generalized public conscience against certain acts of the military that previously might have gone without challenge. For example, there was no courtmartialing of the officers of the *Pueblo*. When a group of soldiers refused an order to go back into murderous enemy gunfire in Viet Nam, the American people did not consider them cowards but sympathized with them. When the trial at the Presidio revealed how harsh and brutal a military court could be, the trial had to be moved elsewhere to avoid further adverse publicity, and the original sentences were drastically reduced. Whatever the whole story is in the case of the Green Berets, part of what went into that government decision was the reaction of the American people to what seemed either arbitrary action by the military or a case of infighting in the military. Television reporting may be slowly influencing the American people to rethink the Viet Nam War in terms of the spirit of the Nuremberg trials.

Other significant signs of a shift in attitude towards war are the high number of appeals to draft boards, and the recognition that a person may be a conscientious objector on nonreligious grounds. We may not at this moment have cracks but we do have fissures. If civilians have the moral right to choose their wars and weapons, we might have turned a major point in the history of the human race.

Section 404: Just War and Atomic War

Until the time of Cicero (106–43 B.C.) war was war. Wars were generally predatory wars or wars of conquest and expansion. No particular justification for war existed and protests against war were short and spasmodic. In his work, *De Officiis*, Cicero tried to work out a rationale for war and spoke of "a righteous ground for going to war" (I, 38). He made other stipulations for right grounds for going to war and condemned wars of covetousness as unjust wars.

Augustine enlarged on the theory of a just war. He lamented that wars do have a terrible aspect but conceded that sometimes good men have to go to war to obtain civic righteousness (*Reply to Faustus*, XXII, 74). In the same work he maintains that wars are righteous when undertaken for righteous reasons. Such reasons are: war for self-defense, war for the cause of civilization, war to inflict punishment, and war to secure reparations. As such, war is for national justice and is not a particularly Christian virtue (*Letter*, 138). Unjust wars are the predatory wars of the barbarians which excite the worst of human passions. The real reason or justifiable reason for war is peace: "Peace should be the object of your desire; war should be waged only as a necessity, and waged only that God may by it deliver men from necessity and preserve them in peace. For peace is not sought in order to be the kindling of war, but war is waged in order that peace may be obtained" (*Letter*, 189). Augustine then lists some of the rules of a just war.

Thomas Aquinas also believed in a just war and ransacked the rules of war specified in the Old Testament as guides for Christians (*Summa Theologica*, I-II, Q. 105, Article 3).

Francisco de Vitoria (c. 1485–1546) is considered by many to be the founder of modern international law and greatly influenced Grotius who is usually considered the founder of international law (1583–1645). In the tradition of Augustine and Thomas, Vitoria defends a just war (translated by Bate in Scott, *The Spanish Origin of International Law*). The one important addition that he made was that a just war had to be fought with just means that would harm neither Christendom nor the world.

Luther wrote a small work (*Ob Kriegesleute auch in seligem Stande sein können* ["Whether Soldiers Too Can Be Saved"], 1526). He states that soldiers may not rebel against their superiors; that they may fight wars with equals for self-defense; that soldiers may war against their own countrymen in obedience to their superiors to put down a rebellion; that there are wars of necessity; and that arbitrary wars are sins.

Calvin said that war was right to execute public vengeance; to defend a state from attack; and to keep the national security (*Institutes of the Christian Religion*, XX, 11).

Grotius is reputedly the founder of the modern idea of a just war in his book, *The Law of War and Peace* (1635). Just wars were wars in self-defense; wars to recover what was legally due a nation; and wars to punish wrongdoing. A war of rebellion was an unjust war.

The Latin text of the Anglican Confession of Faith, *The Thirty-Nine Articles of Religion*, speaks of just wars—*iusta bella*—but the English translation reads "and serve in wars."

In recent literature the idea of the just war drops out and the concept of wars of aggression takes its place (cf. *The Covenant of the League of Nations*, Article 10). In the *Charter of the United Nations* such expressions are used as "acts of aggression," "threats to peace," and "violation of peace."

If all of these documents are sifted through and summed up, a just war must meet the following criteria:

(1) The war must be declared by the proper authority.

(2) There must be a real injury to justify such an action as war.

(3) The damage the war inflicts must not be out of proportion to the original injury.

(4) The war must be fought in a just way.

(5) The war should not be started if it issues in sure defeat with a horrible slaughter of people.

(6) All possible means of negotiation must have failed.

(7) The motive for the party waging war must be right.

The question to be posed is this: *can atomic war be a just war?* Does it fall within or does it fall outside the above criteria?

(1) It has been argued that atomic war is just war in that the death of the enemy is the intent of war and arrows, spears, or bombs are not morally different. Whether a soldier is cremated by an atomic fission or killed with an arrow he is dead, and dead is dead no matter how one arrives there.

(2) It has been argued that atomic war is not just war. The geneticists can predict with some accuracy what a nuclear war would do if it killed the minimum of 100,000,000 people. The radiation and/or other effects of the bomb may not harm the surviving adults too much. But a fetus or a baby is very sensitive to radiation. The damage would be extensive enough so that this part of the surviving population would eventually die. The older generation would then watch the death of the younger and when the older generation died the world would be left with no humanity. If more than 100,000,000 people are killed in the first moments of an atomic war, then the end of the human race is insured just that much more.

A group of scientists calculated what would happen if an atomic bomb were to hit a large city. Among other things, besides hundreds of thousands of deaths, would be the destruction of all public utilities and therefore the uselessness of everything which depended upon them and the destruction of 90 percent of all medical resources—doctors, nurses, hospitals, and medicines. In addition public transportation would cease to exist.

Atomic or nuclear war of any size means, then, the end of humanity directly by its terrible effects and indirectly by its radiation. Further-more these predictions were made *before* there was made known to the public the fact that missiles will carry more than one bomb and can give the scatter-effect similar to the spectacle seen on a fourth of July fireworks display.

Atomic or nuclear war goes beyond all the rules of a just war and can never be called a just war. Our discussion has been restricted to the factor of the end of humanity through one massive nuclear war. But the great number of other lethal and horrible side-effects of nu-clear war are also relevant in deciding if nuclear war is ever a form of just war. Knowing these side effects makes it even more incredible that Christian conscience could ever classify a nuclear war as a just war.

Section 405: Revolution in Values

One of the great Greek dramatists was Aristophanes (448–380 B.C.). In his book, *The Clouds,* we find the generation gap. The father is worried to death about the way his son is carrying on. This is a basic motif of much later literature. In his work, *Steppenwolf* (the "lone" wolf of the steppes), Hermann Hesse (in 1927) sketched out the life of a man out of step with his times. *Steppenwolf* was truly prophetic of the later hippie generation and many hippie slogans as well as hippie prophetic ideas and concepts can be found word for word in *Steppenwolf.* Camus' *The Stranger* is set in North Africa but it too is a description of a young man out of step with his generation. In very recent times Charles Webb's *The Graduate* narrates how the son of a typical middle-class or upper-middle-class couple after graduation from a supposedly safe, ivy-walled college is out of step with his parents and all their friends, and his parents cannot understand his attitudes.

Something happened to the youth of the world after World War II. It is presumed to have started in England and broke out into public attention by the appearance of the Beatles. This movement among the youth of the world, for it is a world-wide phenomenon and not confined either to England or America, is not just more typical youth restlessness. The expression "we thought that way too as kids" is very unrealistic. This is not another typical conflict between children and parents. It is a conflict of such major proportions that it must be thought of more as a revolution.

This movement defies easy description; simple name-calling is ineffectual. It involves a variety of movements with a variety of motifs such as beatniks, hippies, yippies, the New Left, the Third World Revolution, Society for Democratic Action, the Generation Gap, the alienated generation, the beat generation, Black Power, Black Student Union, Brown Power, etc. The enemy, almost as diverse and almost as hard to define, is the Establishment.

An attempt to trace this movement to its ultimate origins as well as present an analysis of the current situation is Lewis Feuer's *The Conflict of Generations.* Simmons and Winograds attempt to describe the inner mentality of the college hippie in *It's Happening.* There is now a large body of literature on the many different phases of the youth revolution. For example, *Religion in Life* (Winter, 1968), devotes to it several articles which attempt to understand the hippie in his historical antecedents and his present mentality ("The Hippies— 1968").

There is no single formula that explains this revolution. It is one of great diversity and contains complex factors. What immediately follows is a list of some of the theories which attempt to explain the various facets of this revolution. Each has its measure of truth and each somehow comes short of being the complete explanation.

(1) The affirmation of men like Nietzsche and Spengler, to name but two, was that Western culture had reached its end. The old synthesis had collapsed. Western culture was an old animal wandering around for a soft place to lie down and die. A new era was being born. The new creature-culture was emerging. Superman was coming.

The prophecies were right but the timing was wrong. Not in 1900 or 1918 but in the 1960s the age of Aquarius came. So we are now going through the death throes of an old culture and the birth pangs of a new one.

(2) The "rapidization" theory is that cultural change is going on at atomic speeds. Modern youth must go through changes in ten years that heretofore took a thousand years. He is pushed too fast and so hard that he can't cope with it. He is literally unhinged. His drugs, his music, his politics, and his protests represent his ill-digested, ill-conceived efforts to cope with so rapid a change of culture which no generation of man should have to cope with. But whether they like it

or not, these young people have no choice. They have been smitten with rapidization.

(3) The vector theory is similar to the rapidization theory. It affirms that our present generation of young people is being bombarded from many sides with factors of great pressure: the new physics; the new astronomy; space explorations; the knowledge explosion; the paperback explosion; the end of old colonial empires and the birth of new nations; the new pattern of police wars; and brinkmanship diplomacy! The speed of change is so great that it is jokingly said that a physicist at the age of thirty is an old man in science. Like the rapidization theory the vector theory says that human beings cannot cope with so many factors converging on them at once. The younger generation can't vector the vectoring. The sum of all its odd behavior is the only way it feels that the pressure of the vectoring process can be reduced.

(4) The atomic bomb theory is harder to pin down. It is not easy to see how the bomb directly influences young people. But the theory states that at the unconscious level young people feel that at any time nuclear warfare could end it all. This has the effect of foreshortening their entire scheme of life. They think in terms of five years not fifty years. So their sex, their literature, their movies, their drugs, and their bohemian ways are so-called five year plans. In a nuclear age who can think more than five years at a time?

(5) The Communist plot theory is that whereas a direct war upon the United States is not possible, systematic undermining of America is. Not all youth movements are Communist inspired or masterminded. But they are all taken advantage of by the Communists who finance, aggravate, and attempt to give further direction to the movement. What Russia cannot do with guns and bombs she can do through clever manipulation of our youth.

(6) The basic cause is the state of our universities. In many instances they have become too large. Schools built for a few thousand students must now educate tens of thousands of students. Specialized seminars designed for ten people now contain a hundred. The student is an IBM card. Some colleges contact their students for school business only by telephone or letter. Otherwise the offices would be glutted with students. Important or famous professors are never seen. The professor is on a specialized research project and must forego teaching; or he limits his teaching to a seminar of a few superior students; or he

145

is doing research or teaching in some other country; or he is living on airplanes serving as consultant to several different companies. The student ends up with a schedule made up of oversized classes taught by inferior instructors.

Besides that, the student suspects a duplicity in the university. The sociology department knows the evils of the city in which the university is located but does nothing about it. The political science department knows the machinations of the state government but does nothing to expose them. The philosophy department has a course or two on ethics but the lectures have a paper taste divorced from the realities of student life. The science and engineering departments are not doing pure research but doing government research for the military or for big industry. The trustees are usually men over sixty in the $100,-000 a year bracket, and are usually more concerned with maintaining their economic empires than running a truly academic university.

The students find themselves in a quandary. After a student riot the general public learns that many petitions sent through normal university channels were ignored, or handed back with some vague reason for rejecting them scribbled on them by an apparently hurried and disinterested person. Interviews or consultations were ineffectual. What course was left for the students? The answer is a very traditional one in university history: *violence*. In this way their voice is heard and the university is forced to recognize what the students are attempting to say. The contemporary university is thereby forced to come to terms with the state of the modern world.

(7) The "knowledge explosion theory" claims that the modern student knows about ten times more than his father knew when he went to university. The avalanche of paperback books has permitted the old system of one text per course to give way to a sheaf of paperbacks per course. Disregarding inflation the student's book bill per term is two or three times that of his parents in their days at the university. In addition there are national journals with in-depth reporting plus the more radical kind of newspaper and the underground newspaper. The very nature of the situation makes a reliable figure impossible to obtain. But it is estimated that the reading audience of underground newspapers may run as high as ten million. Daily television programs of the news or interview variety put live public figures directly before the eyes of the students.

The time gap and the distance gap and the personality gap are now all bridged in one way or another. The modern student knows the ills of society in great detail and sees the failures to deal with them. Students react in mass with a righteous indignation to such ills. In their fathers' day only a few highly politically activated students did anything out of the way. The typical "Joe College" or "Fraternity Jim" of a past generation has given way to a very articulate, very culturally sensitive person.

(8) The McLuhan theory is that we now have the first television generation in college. Each medium of news or information has a way of shaping the recipient of that news. The unique thing about television is that it "sucks" the listener into the situation. He wants to be a reactor and a participator as well as a listener and a learner. He wants to form policy in the university, be on committees, and help choose faculty members. Our television generation does not want to be docile readers or listeners; television makes them participators. So the modern student demands his say in education, in science, in business, and in politics.

(9) This is the unspanked generation, the Dewey generation. People over fifty remember the whippings in the woodshed. A modern child has never seen a woodshed. The modern furnace has replaced it. People over fifty also remember the spanking arsenal of the principal. He had his piece of garden hose or array of paddles. Some of these paddles had holes in them to cut down the air resistance of the swing. Other principals used parts of broken baseball bats. Educators believed in the value of the spanking; the students expected it as part of student life; and parents approved of the spanking if they felt their youngster had stepped out of line and therefore had it coming.

When education became excessively pupil-centered, when the educators thought one learned by doing and not by thinking, when permissiveness replaced discipline, the result has been a generation without fiber—spoiled, ego-centered, undisciplined. They do not have proper respect or fear of parents, educators, or policemen. They are not intimidated by threats of punishment. They want to solve their problems their way, to express their opinions their way, and to understand law enforcement their way. "Law and order" is really the tyranny of the Establishment.

(10) This is the soft generation. They have never had to learn how to live with less and less as in a time of depression. They have never learned to repair, invent, or improvise. They have not learned to be

147

three seasons back in their clothes. They have never faced the national and international threat of an Emperor William or a Hitler. Abraham Low, a psychiatrist, believes very strongly that our way of educating youth has terribly weakened and softened them so that they are a gutless and willess generation. Our way of instructing them in how to use machines, making them so dependent on labor-saving devices, and teaching them to solve all their problems by running to a specialist when the first sharp pain hits them has contributed to their present condition (*Mental Health,* pp. 135–40).

(11) This is the naïve generation. The young generation charges the older generation with hypocrisy. The older generation condemns drugs yet gulps pills by the handful; it demands discipline yet has its drinking parties that become rowdy; it tells children to be honest yet it cheats every way it can in business and against the government; it speaks with respect for the church yet ignores Christian ethics in business. But the older generation affirms that this is the way it has to be and to think otherwise is to be naïve. The older folk know that society has to have an ethical front, a common moral wall of restraints. But it also knows that there is some devil in all of us. Fudging one way or another is part of the reality of life. Nobody is really being deceived into thinking that one thing is demanded and another is done. This is not regarded as hypocritical but part of the way that imperfect people have to live with each other.

There must be a standard of law or morality for society to hang together, yet economic and social survival means that there will always be some breaking of the law within the law. The new generation that wants ethics and practice to match, are green and naïve about the rough and tumble of life. To attempt to cure society or hypocrisy reveals a poorly digested view of society and an unrealistic assessment of human nature. Certainly in an abstract way hypocrisy is a sin, but unfortunately sinners can live only with a certain amount of hypocrisy. This demand for purism, for consistency, for lack of hypocrisy, and this condemnation of double talk are demands of young people who are yet green, immature, and naïve about the rough and tough way this world of sinners and imperfect people must function.

The articles and books on these kinds of problems form an endless stream. Our concern is with the ethics of the situation and how the ethical issues affect the church. The attitude of the younger generation towards the church contains some of the following elements:

(1) The church is with the Establishment and against the young people when it comes to basic ethical issues. This word "Establishment" is a conglomerate. It can mean any person who is above any group of young people and gives them orders or controls them. Or it can mean anybody or any group of people over thirty. Or it can mean a teacher, a principal, a dean, a president, a policeman, a congress, a governor, or a social worker. But it means "the old guard," the "ancient regime," or the "dated generation." Ethically the church is in harmony with the Establishment.

(2) The church lets the roof fall in before it moves. The classic example is that the churches of the South let racism develop in its ugliest features and did nothing about it until the black people were forced into violent means of protesting to break up a pattern of systematic suppression.

(3) The minister is a paid man. How can he be prophetic or critical? He works with the Establishment or he is out. In fairness to the ministry it must be said that not all churches have the same financial arrangement with the ministry so that in a number of denominations the pastor's salary is not threatened if he becomes prophetic.

(4) Ethically speaking the church is conservative, reactionary, and dead on its feet. It goes along with a system of morals and values that is dated. It accepts the political and economic system as it is without any sense of the injustices that permeate the system.

Right or wrong this is generally how the younger generation feels about the church.

Our interpretation of the situation is that we are as a Western culture, as an American nation, and as a Christian church facing a crisis or revolution in morals and values, particularly in values. Here is the real rub between the church and the younger generation.

The basic clash in America between parents and children has been cultural. Parents from Poland or Spain or Russia maintained as much as they could in their homes the mother tongue and the old world culture. Their children were in a public school system learning English and playing with American children and learning American culture. It is an old story which has been the theme of numerous movies, plays, novels, and radio dramas. The culture clash has not vanished. Such situations still exist but they are now a minor phenomenon.

The present clash is the value clash. The most obvious description of it is in *The Graduate*. Mother and father and their friends live according to one set of values; the son lives according to another. They misunderstand each other; shoot past each other; and talk around each other. The parents cannot see that their son is operating under a different set of values so they completely misunderstand him. *The Graduate* represents just one slice of the value clash, so let us now look at the whole spectrum:

(1) The modern generation wants a new understanding of sexual morality. It wants to bring ethics and practice together. We have discussed the new permissiveness at another point and it need not be belabored here. We only wish to point out that sexual values are part of the remaking of a new code of ethics and values. Marriages of convenience, marriages of toleration, marriages of economic necessity, marriages for social advantage, and marriages for business advantage all betray a corrupted sense of the real values in human sexuality. Maybe a new kind of communal marriage would restore the proper values.

(2) The modern generation wants a new intimacy in personal relationships. Recently there have been mass meetings of tens of thousands of young people with no violence or demonstration. The desire of the same kind to be together with their kind of music was the organizing factor. Technology, industry, and mass everything create the "lonely crowd." The *pad* concept has come into existence. This is a group of like-minded young people simply spending an evening or a night together. Unfortunately it is seen too frequently as an adventure in sex or drugs or alcohol, but the real motivation is deeper, namely, finding community in a world of the impersonal. The sort of thing the Establishment calls socialization is too conventional, too trite, and has too much gamesmanship in it. There is almost a Rousseau touch here of going back to the unspoiled primitive in the new ethic of community among young people.

(3) The modern generation wants education for life. The necessity of science and mathematics and long hours in laboratory work is not denied. But in courses where life ought to encounter life, one should not be faced with dull lectures, duller textbooks, and terribly passé theories and attitudes. There should be fewer impersonal relationships in our universities, less research for the prestige of research, less publication for earning merit badges in the academic community, and fewer connections with the business and industrial world. There should be more interaction with community problems, social problems,

personal problems, and political problems. There should be more sub-
jectivity (in the good sense) in education and less objectivity (in the
bad sense) in our universities.

(4) The modern generation wants an ethic that puts a real human
being in the center of ethical concern. The commercial world should
be less dog-eat-dog. Competition should not be soul-destroying as so
much of it is. The business world, the industrial world, the commercial
world, and the banking world, should never sacrifice persons, rights,
and humanity for gain.

The most recent manifestation of social indignation with the young
generation has been in ecology. They abhor the destruction of natural
resources, natural beauty, and the corruption of rivers, streams, and
oceans by a greedy industry and insatiable capitalism. The more mature and academic expression of this value revolution is expressed in
the articles by scholars in *The Center Magazine* published by the
Center for the Study of Democratic Institutions (Santa Barbara, California).

(5) The modern generation wants authenticity in life. They don't
want to surrender their individuality and freedom to the controlled
life of a big corporation. To work with a big corporation a man has
to be married to the right wife, live in the right community, go to the
right church, belong to the right lodge, and be free from obvious vices.
If he conforms to these criteria, he is allowed to move up the ladder
of promotions and end up in the big house in the exclusive residential
district and belong to the right country club. He does all of this not
to express himself and his individuality, but to get somewhere. And
in getting somewhere he loses himself.

So the hippie cuts out of society. He does what he wants to do. He
does his thing. He may eat more beans than steak, and wear jeans
rather than a suit, but at least he is himself. He is nobody's lackey and
he is his own master. What he lacks in creature comforts and security
he gains in selfhood. He feels that being authentic is much more important than being a success in a corporation.

(6) The modern generation wants authentic religion. On the surface
they appear antichurch and antireligion, but in reality they are re-
ligiously sensitive. They look more towards mysticism, meditation, ori-
ental religions, and music rather than conforming to typical denominational life. They are willing to go with new music and new liturgies
in the older churches but not with the old preaching, the old hymns,

the old appeals, the old clichés, and the old ethics. Some may be atheistic or militantly antireligious but this is a part and not the whole. Some churches have actually gone to a pattern of two services—a conventional one for the older people and the "pop mass" for the college student.

(7) In their new humanism the modern generation is pacifistic and antimilitary.

(8) They are the *now* generation. As indicated the present international chaos and threat of nuclear war has shortened their value system. They do not buy the long haul value systems of their parents. They don't believe in delayed action for future returns. The essence of stupidity is getting a gold watch for thirty years of dog-like loyalty to a company. Their values are *now* values, experiential values. They want immediacy in experience and pleasure and reward. This drives them to sex *now*, trips *now*, and novel experiences *now*.

The music they want is music they can feel. After listening to some records with a group of college students I asked them about the significance of some of the words. The reply I got was "It's the beat, not the words." That is why the drummer is the center of the combo. He sets and controls the beat. However, this is not entirely true as the words do express the general scheme of values and types of experiences that the younger generation is after. Furthermore much of their political and social ideology comes out in their ballads. But when a group really works up a storm, the beat and the high magnification of the sound by electrical help obscure the words and whatever genuine aesthetic elements are in the music.

This means that they believe in spontaneity. They look for a "happening." They want to hang free from conventions. The canned and the planned have no existential spark.

(9) The modern generation values the individuality of each person in his own unique feelings and needs. This means an attitude of freedom and tolerance toward every other person. Each person has the right to do his own thing. There is no necessity for a person to conform to standards of the past in such areas as drama, movies, novels, art, or dance. One expresses his own mood, feelings, attitudes, spirit, perspective, and even his own interpretation rather than conforming to conventional rules of art whether classical or modern.

This idea is also expressed by the modern generation in their theory of law. They maintain that there should be no laws concerning what consenting adults do in the privacy of their homes and results in no harm to other people. To do one's thing, a kind of popularization of Sartre's philosophy, should not be subject to law if it is not hurting another person or society. Laws should be concerned with matters in which people hurt each other. If a trip with a drug in somebody's pad gives a person a real experience and hurts nobody else, there should be no law against that kind of use of the drug. If a person drives a car while drunk and kills somebody that is a matter which belongs to law.

What can be said about such a new system of values? Is it revolutionary? destructive of society? or the beginning of a new era of true humanism and authenticity? However society decides, certain restraining comments are pertinent:

(1) There is a difference between ideals and the means of achieving ideals. The Establishment may feel that the ideal of the hippie is right but the means of achieving it is wrong. The Black Panthers may have a real case for justice but default by the wrong means. As much thinking must go into the means of achieving ends as thinking about the right ends in the first place. The wrong means may postpone the achievement of the right ends for decades. Reactions and backlashes are also realities of life.

(2) There is a real danger in oversimplification. The older generation may recognize genuine criticism in what the younger set is saying, but the younger set is too easily the victim of the big oversimplification. For example:

Life on this earth is impossible without compromise at many points. Universities can exist only within a texture of compromises, and any university the New Left would establish would have its own rash of compromises. They would just be in a different direction or of a different type. A city without a police force is an impossibility. The police action in a city is simply not one uniform pig activity. Not all parents are playing a systematic game of hypocrisy by telling their children one thing and doing another. Not all university trustees are members of the John Birch Society. Not all churches are mere echoes of the values and mores of the Establishment. Not every politician is a pork-barrel, logrolling type. There are some oases of integrity.

Let us put the shoe on the other foot. If the New Left and organizations similar to it were to take over the government tomorrow, Utopia would not begin. They would have their problems, their inequalities, their injustices, their quota of pigs, and their share of vices.

Historically old problems, old vices, old inefficiencies, and old divisions always come back to haunt the new revolution. We would be cynics and pessimists if we did not believe that there was a substantial stock of idealism in the human race; we would be simpletons and fools if we thought that with the advance of idealism problems vanish as the morning mist before the noonday sun.

(3) There is also the danger of being ahistorical. By ahistorical we mean that the contemporary generation gets so preoccupied with its present problems it fails to take a hard look at history. As the old saying goes, those who do not learn from history are condemned to repeat it. *Something* in the past gave the hippie his supposedly new insight. *Something* in education of the past makes the student of the present unhappy about his education. *Something* of the past has given us our present technology. *Something* of the past has given us the sense of criticism of the present. To negate the past is but to show blindness, stupidity, and prejudice against some of the very forces that give our generation its superior insights. The essential kernel of truth is classicalism and cannot be controverted. Every age stands on the shoulders of the previous ages and to this degree deserves some measure of respect.

(4) Eventually the New Left and the younger generation must come to terms with the realities of life. Many hippies are supported by parents on the grounds that sending their hippie children money is at least *one* tie with them. These parents feel that if they stop the monthly check, all will be lost for sure.

But the young generation eventually marry. The bills do come in. When a baby is born the couple discover they have an expensive item on their hands. Eventually mother or father has a cavity or two that needs dental attention. The car wears out or breaks down. The little family has to live in some kind of house.

Until the new order comes the New Left has to live within the terms of the old order. That is why the population of the New Left and of the hippie crowd begins to drop off drastically after age 25. Idealism has had to come to grips with realism. Criticism has to bend its knee to economics. The protestor has to have that weekly pay check. The world of white and black has become gray; and the disjunctives of right and wrong have buckled into necessary compromise. It would be a complete misunderstanding of the above paragraphs to interpret the expression "the realities of life" as a clever propaganda statement to force the newer generation to give in to the mores, values, and patterns of the Establishment.

That the younger generation is making its impact upon the traditional way of life in America cannot be denied. Their excesses can lead to correctives. "Make love not war" is a serious attempt to call our society back to a genuine humanitarianism. The refusal to join the economic ladder in the big corporation is a reminder to us that it is better to be our real selves and poor, than financial successes made at the expense of our genuine freedom. Their attack on police methods and the courts could be a serious reminder that our juridical system has been steadily drifting away from the ideals which originally created it. Their by-passing of the church can be a sharp reprimand to the church that it is too selective in the cross-section of society to which it appeals and too traditional, doctrinaire, and professional in what it says via the pulpit. So even if the New Left has to "rejoin" the Establishment, it is not the old Establishment but one already set in motion for correctives initiated by the younger generation. Comically the "old" Establishment is becoming the "new" Establishment because many of the New Left generation are *now* practicing lawyers, doctors, politicians, and businessmen!

Section 406: Changing Society

The American presupposition has been that the way to change law, government, or society was by proper democratic procedures. But this assumption is now no longer held by many segments within our American society.

(1) Some groups think that in any issue the problem revolves around what is right and what is wrong. The democratic procedure may not only fail to produce the right but actually defeat it. Therefore some groups feel that they have a right to recourse to nondemocratic procedures. If all the democratic procedures do not produce what they feel is right in a given controversy over wages, working conditions, and fringe benefits then they feel that they do not have to abide by democratic process but have a right to strike.

For example, suppose a group of teachers believe that they should be paid a certain salary. The board of education goes through all the democratic procedures that it should and comes up with a figure below the expectation of the teachers. Although democratic procedures have been followed by the board, the teachers do not feel bound to the decision of the board. They decide that *their* idea of what is right is more important than the democratic procedure of the board and so the teachers strike. The theory is then that a group is to stick to what it thinks is right, not what the democratic procedure produces; and if the democratic procedure does not come up to expectations, the group has a moral right to strike.

(2) Or there is the conviction that the democratic process itself has failed. It seems that governments respond more to pressures than to votes; or that they respond more to vested interests than to needs of people; or that politicians have to make so many debts to be elected that they are bought men. It is common knowledge that it takes millions of dollars to be elected mayor of a city, tens of millions of dollars to be elected governor of a state, and another astronomical sum to be elected president. The democratic process cannot work if politicians have to pay off so many political debts.

It has come to light in a number of student riots that a whole series of democratic maneuvers by the students were ignored. The democratic process was overridden by the administration. The black community has found that usual forms of democracy or protest do not get results. There are two questions: has the democratic process become generally inoperative? And, if society is too sick to be cured by resort to usual democratic processes, how do we change society?

(1) *Quietism.* The Quietist believes that the world is the devil's possession. On the surface a society may seem to run itself by democracy or conformity to law, but in the background lurks the Evil One. Efforts at change are unrealistic. Man is too depraved or too sinful to make any real change for righteousness. To be specific, what kind of legislation about the control of liquor can come from a group of politicians who drink?

Or, Quietism may be built on the theory of a strong separation of state and church. The church has no real business in politics. The Christian obligation is discharged by voting the best ticket possible in any given election. Unfortunately the Quietist is not aware of the fact that many of the rights he enjoys were bought by the blood of non-Quietists.

(2) *Change-the-Heart Theory.* It has been maintained that morality cannot be legislated. Good men give us good government, so the

aim of the Christian is to get good men into office and millions of good men into the voting booths. Therefore the real way to change society is to change the hearts of its citizens. Wesley's revival work in England is the case most frequently cited. If it were not for his revivals the English would have gone the way of the French Revolution. This theory proposes that in America today the only real answer to poverty problems, racial problems, and international problems is a great religious revival. Out of this would come enough people with changed hearts to change society.

Because so many evangelical people believe in the changed heart theory, it must be more critically examined. Relevant to this discussion is C. F. H. Henry's book, *Aspects of Christian Social Ethics,* in which he as an evangelical discusses the ways and means of social change (along with a discussion of other items of Christian social ethics).

(i) At the present rates of growth in general population and church membership the percentage of Christians in the American population is shrinking. The Christian community in America is getting smaller and smaller in comparison to the size of the total community. This works strongly against the change-the-heart theory.

At the present time the only evangelist who draws the thousands into his meetings is Billy Graham. He has had many remarkable conversions in his services and these people in turn have exerted a strong influence in their particular spheres. But the population in America is so large and the problems so massive that the church needs a thousand men like Billy Graham to make the kinds of changes that are necessary. In the days when labor unions were fighting for their existence many people within the Christian church and many church organizations supported labor. It has been calculated that the effect of the church on the situation was 2 percent. It is a statistic like this that leads one to the conviction that the change-the-heart theory needs at least a thousand Billy Grahams to insure significant social change.

(ii) There is no automatic change of heart in political or economic attitude when a person is converted. Many converts retain their old prejudices. The church historian knows of too many evils and injustices perpetrated by people whose hearts are supposed to have been changed. John Swain's *A History of Torture* reveals that the people in the church with changed hearts were just as barbarous in their practices of torture as the people whose hearts were unchanged. The assurances so frequently given from the pulpit that if we can change enough hearts we will change society cannot be entirely believed. There is no necessary or automatic connection at this point.

(iii) More is needed in our present situation than changed hearts. There must be just programs and righteous policies. A person in high places with a changed heart may be utterly confused about which program is right, fair, and just. The changed heart may change values, ethics, and perspectives but it may be as ignorant as any other heart about what the actual law or practice ought to be to make for righteousness.

(iv) Finally changed hearts don't pull down unrighteous walls. This is the hardest point to get across to people who believe in the changed-heart theory. If a union refuses to accept black people as apprentices, where do we go from here? If we wait for the leaders of the union to become Christians, the blacks might have to wait a hundred years for changes in union policy. To tell minority groups that they will get the right treatment when more of the majority group becomes Christian is not going to make much of an impression.

Or take another situation. If a company hires one-third of its employees from minority groups, these people usually end up with jobs at the bottom of the pile where advancement is either impossible or very restricted. Are these people to be told that when the administration becomes Christian *then* their problems will be solved and that their strategy is to await the conversion of management?

(v) Historically speaking many theologians have believed that a theory of Christian politics and economics is necessary in addition to a changed-heart theory such as the theology of common grace, or the concept of a Christian civilization, or some concept of church and state. Thus the Christian correctives are built into the system from the ground up. Whether they work or not is another question. But at least it must be recognized that a number of Christian theologians long before there was a "social gospel" had a positive theory of the method whereby Christian ethical norms become part of the ethical norms of society too.

(3) *The Law and Order Theory*. This group believes that change ought to come where there is injustice but that all change must be by law and order. This has been set forth recently in a competent form by former Justice Fortas, *Concerning Dissent and Civil Disobedience*.

There are many forms of protest available to the American citizen (and student)—letters, petitions, sit-ins, marches, rallies, etc. But dissent should never involve destruction of property and harm to people. Protest may be strong, militant, vigorous, and persistent, but never contrary to law and order. In this way people may make it clear that the democratic process is failing somewhere. This is presumably the method approved by the great silent middle-class majority in America.

(4) *Violence*. Some political ideologies believe that violence is part of social change. The old guard holds on to its way of life very tenaciously and only violence breaks it away.

But why are those people violent who have no such basic theory of violence? Why should a group of students take over the research laboratory of a university when as a group they have no articulate theory of violence? Why should a black community resort to violence when upon questioning it is ascertained that they have no socialistic or communistic or anarchistic political background that would teach them violence as one form of making social change?

The answer to such questions is a pragmatic one: *violence works*. Fifty petitions may be sent to the administration of a school and *nothing* happens. Burn down a building, toss a couple of bombs, kidnap the dean—something happens. Or, the blacks may point to many efforts to obtain change in their community. Nothing happens. But after a riot that destroys about $50,000,000 worth of property the city fathers suddenly start to make changes. If we want to be historical we can refer to the origin of the United States. *The Declaration of Independence* (July 4, 1776) is from the literary standpoint a very polished document. But buried beneath this fine rhetoric is the threat of violence—"we pledge to each other our lives, our fortunes, and our sacred honor." Only by resort to violence did we become independent from England. Or, examine Patrick Henry's famous speech, "The War Inevitable, March, 1775." There is no mistaking the note of violence in his famous concluding line: "I know not what course others may take; but as for me, give me liberty or give me death!" And how was that death to come save from violent opposition to the British?

Or a review may be made of the history of revolution or rebellion in Christian ethics. It is surprising how many Christian theologians believed that when the state ceased to function as the state according to Holy Scripture the citizenry had a right to revolt.

But the problem involved with justifying violence to solve a problem is similar to that of a just war. No just war may be started *if* it is going to end in a great blood bath. The basic reason why millions of people submit to communism behind the Iron Curtain is that any significant opposition is going to result in a great bloodshed. The nations behind the Iron Curtain feel that it is a lesser evil to live with communism than it is to start a movement that could end in the death of millions of their fellow citizens. So when any group resorts to violence it must always calculate the best it can the possible losses as well as the gains it sees so clearly. Or to express it another way, the battle may be won and the war lost. Violence in our cities and schools may win a battle but lose a war. The battle won at the school board may be lost at the ballot box with its bond issues. Those who resort to violence to solve a problem because it seems to work and it seems to thaw out the democratic process must not do so without considering very soberly the important and necessary distinction between winning battles and losing wars. During the Revolutionary War America gambled. It not only won the battles; it won the war. The South gambled. It won some significant battles but lost the war. Hitler gambled. For a period of time he ruled Europe from Moscow through North Africa. His troops won many brilliant battles but they lost the war. Any resort to violence must be seen as a gamble.

Society can be changed many ways. In human history many theories of change have worked. At other times they have failed. Therefore any attempt to change society must be preceded by "the big think" in which is assessed not only what changes may be immediately won but what also may be lost when the action is viewed from the perspective of years. Concerning the possibility of making real changes in society three different opinions have been held:

(1) *Pessimists.* Pessimists believe that man is too corrupt, or that the force of evil is too great in the universe, and no real change can be made. Technological improvement is not really the same thing as the betterment of man. In fact an educated and technologically trained devil is worse than an ignorant Stone Age devil. The boasted betterment of man is really illusory.

Christians may be pessimists on two scores: (i) They may believe that the doctrine of total depravity teaches us that no matter what material or scientific progress man makes he will still be an immoral sinner; or (ii) they may argue eschatologically and cite those passages which indicate that when Christ returns things will be in their worst possible condition, not their best.

(2) *Optimists.* From Plato's *Republic* until today men have been writing about Utopia. It is ironical that the Greek word *Utopia* means "no where" (*ou* and *topos*). But there have always been philosophers or politicians or religionists who believe that by God's grace, the Spirit's power, or man's intelligence all the bad kinks in society will be straightened out and some sort of ideal condition will prevail on earth. Christian postmillennialists have been accused of being optimists as well as religious liberals and humanists.

(3) *Meliorism.* Some philosophers and theologians do not believe that things are going to get better or worse by some sort of law, natural, theological, or sociological. Man makes his own way. He can make it worse; he can make it better. *Meliorism* (from the Greek word for better) believes that if mankind uses its good sense, its good judgment, and its science it can make things better even if it cannot create Utopia. The term *Meliorism* was coined by George Eliot (1819–1880) but the idea was made popular by the American philosopher, William James (1842–1910). Most people are Meliorists. They resist the gloomy view of the pessimist's universe and believe the opinions of the Utopians to be unrealistic.

Section 407: Business Ethics

The Harvard School of Business conducted a survey to find out how much help the pastor and the local church gave the businessman in making his ethical decisions in the business world. The results were very discouraging. Only 20 percent of the businessmen claimed to have received any kind of help at all.

Yet the whole population as buyer or consumer is involved with the business world. Why is there such little advice from the church about an activity that concerns every single member of a congregation except the younger children?

Perhaps the minister's education has been so much in liberal arts and theology that he has no background to make significant ethical interpretations in business.

Perhaps the minister has so many other topics he wishes to speak on that he never gets around to business ethics.

Perhaps the businessman never goes out of his way to look up the pastor and ask him his advice on business ethics.

Perhaps the minister is very evangelical and thinks speaking on business ethics would give the impression that he believed in the Social Gospel.

Perhaps the business world is so complex that ethical interpretations are difficult to make.

Perhaps the competition in the business world is so tough that the businessman must forget about ethics and concentrate on surviving.

Perhaps the business world is condemned to grays and moral ambiguities.

There is one question this section will not debate: *is there an economic system more just than the one we live under in America?* Of course the real ethical question about business is what form of economics brings the most justice to people. Our concern is to discuss the issue where we are, namely, *how business is now being practiced.* Two books which are within the grasp of the layman are of real help here. M. W. Childs' *Ethics in a Business Society* is basically a historical review that brings us up to the present. H. A. Gram's *The Christian Encounters Ethics and Social Responsibility in Business* is written from a Christian perspective and discusses business ethics as business is now practiced in America.

In discussing business ethics there are three matters which must come first:

(1) Customers demand that certain items be sold a certain way which forces the businessman into practices that he does not approve but his only recourse is to appease the customer.

Anthony Till has spent his life in the world of selling cars (*What You Should Know Before You Buy a Car*) and we use his experience as typical of the way so many other products are sold.

Till conducted an experiment of his own. For a period of time he sold cars as honestly as he could. He told the customers all the facts and used not one trade gimmick. His sales dropped to almost zero.

Then he took another chunk of time and modified his approach. Along with his honest approach he mixed in a few of the typical sales tricks of the business. He sold more cars but not the usual amount.

Finally he went back to selling cars with all the ruses of salesmanship and his sales returned to normal. The moral is that the customer wanted the car sold to him a certain way. Many practices which might be considered unethical are not the choices of the merchants but reflect the manner in which people want to purchase things. The problems in business ethics are then obviously not those stemming only from the merchant but many are forced upon the businessman by the customer.

(2) The second consideration is the location of the responsibility. A merchant can sell only what he in turn can buy. If he can buy only cheap or defective merchandise then that is the only kind he can sell. From the time a product is but a raw material until it is an item on sale in a store, a whole chain of events has occurred. To pinpoint the blame in the production of inferior merchandise would take a research team.

(3) According to Gram there are seven things which the American people expect from business: (i) to do what it can to eliminate depressions; (ii) to help in the rebuilding of cities; (iii) to assist in the location of diseases that plague a city; (iv) to give financial aid to college education; (v) to aid in wiping out poverty; (vi) to eliminate racial prejudice in its total operation; and (vii) to control pollution. These are the social responsibilities which the American public expects from large corporations.

The *obvious* culprit is not necessarily the *real* culprit. Reinhold Niebuhr's *An Interpretation of Christian Ethics* contains some scathing criticisms against theologians of the liberal orientation. He says that they do not reckon with the complexity of the business world and therefore have an idealism of the business world that is irrelevant for the practices of that world.

Writers on the ethics of business have pointed out some of the more obvious areas in which business and industry need to sharpen up or tighten up their ethical practices such as:

(1) Industry must face the problem of pollution of all sorts more realistically than it has in the past. This is a vast area for further ethical exploration—the "ecology explosion."

(2) Industry must show responsibility for the use of natural resources not only with regard for coming generations but also with regard to present destruction to the balance of nature.

(3) Business and industry must also reckon with the emotional damage they may do to people. At the present the central concern has been with the physical safety of the worker. But practices in management may create serious emotional problems for the worker. Arthur Miller attempted to call attention to this kind of emotional damage in his play, *The Death of a Salesman.*

Another facet of the same problem is a real concern among college youth. They fear that to work for a corporation they must *conform* to social and personal practices dictated by the corporation. They fear being made into corporation images rather than being allowed to mature into their authentic selves.

(4) Corporations must act responsibly towards their community in making any major change that will affect the lives of thousands of people (such as relocation).

(5) The American people are unaware of the image of "economic imperialism" American corporations create in other countries. In fact American "economic imperialism" in foreign countries may do more to encourage communistic activities than the poverty of the people. Economic imperialism is, if not the chief source, at least a principle cause of feelings of ill will toward America in the world. Therefore American corporations must have policies which show ethical sensitivity and responsibility toward the countries in which they operate.

(6) Management and labor must come into more and more of a sense of responsibility and act accordingly with respect to the effect of their practices, relationships, wages, and prices on millions of American people. The present rash of inflationary contracts is unethical in respect to the millions of poor people, retired people, and fixed-income people who have no way of solving the problem of the inflated prices created by inflationary contracts.

(7) Industry must become more conscientious towards the potential harm of the products or the lack of safety features in their products. For example, we know that automobiles can be manufactured with far more safety factors built into them than they now have.

(8) More and more American people feel that built-in obsolescence of products is unethical. They are coming to believe that it is unethical to make slight changes in older models with the obvious intent of making the older model look dated when the difference between the models is really insignificant.

(9) Dishonesty in advertising is not ethically justifiable and it is expected that the American public will eventually strongly protest this feature of business practice.

(10) There are many practices in salesmanship that are blatantly unethical. Perhaps at the top of the list is overselling the customer. The man who can afford only a $2,000 car may be coaxed into spending

$2,500 to $3,000. A customer who can afford only a house in the $15,000 to $18,000 range is talked into buying a $25,000 house.

(11) Packaging of products that is deceiving is also ethically wrong. There are a thousand variations on this theme. For a concrete example, consider the inflationary repricing of an article which is cleverly concealed by novel packaging. The customer is deceived into thinking that he is getting the old product at the old price.

(12) There is another commonly practiced unethical trick. Goods are sold with the trade label of a good product, but in actuality the merchandise is a cheaper version of the real product manufactured solely for the special sale. This is pure deception.

As previously indicated some of these sharp practices are really the fault of the customer. He wants the merchandise sold to him in a way that is really unethical. So not all sharp practices are the dictates of business. Perhaps the most disturbing item of all in the world of business and industry is that the major thievery in the United States does not involve goods stolen by professional thieves but goods taken by employees of the store or factory.

What can the church do about business?

(1) One of the most promising developments is that various schools of business and businessmen's groups are inviting professors of Christian ethics to give their analyses of the function of ethics in business.

Community service clubs should welcome local pastors to lead discussions concerning ethical dimensions in business.

(2) The ministerial fellowship of a town, community, or city could be progressive and aggressive in inviting businessmen to periodic seminars on the relationship of the Christian ethic to business. This should be carefully and professionally done with adequate preparation by the ministers. These ministers could also sponsor the coming of some informed person in Christian ethics to lecture or to be the resource person for such a seminar.

(3) Seminars on Christian faith and business ethics can be held within a local church if it is large enough to have a significant attendance. Here pastors, deacons, elders, and Christian businessmen (and professional men too!) can talk over the problems of being a Christian (a moral man) in the business world (an immoral society—with regards to Niebuhr's *Moral Man and Immoral Society*).

(4) There is another side to business ethics and that is how the Christian layman can be helped in avoiding the unethical practices in

the business world. The stewardship of life includes the stewardship of our money, and the wise spending of money is as much a part of Christian stewardship as giving to the church. The most effective means of putting an end to unethical business practices is an informed public that knows how to shop critically and intelligently.

(5) The church can be a resource for information and instruction in business ethics. If businessmen complain that the church does not help them, then it means that the preaching and teaching ministry of the church has skirted business ethics. The only remedy is to pull business ethics into preaching and into teaching. If all sorts of personal, social, and political matters are dealt with as ethical issues, why should business go neglected? The preaching and teaching ministry should be backed up by a library or literature ministry. There is a wealth of written material on Christian business ethics.

Section 408: The Senior Citizen

Thanks to modern surgery and medicines millions of people today are alive in their seventies and eighties who a few decades ago would have died in their fifties and sixties. The unexpected result is that the second largest segment of our population is composed of people over 65 and in a decade will number ten percent of our population.

The United States Department of Health, Education, and Welfare is publishing a magazine called *Aging* to help elderly people solve the problems typical of their age. The Greek word for an old man is *gerōn* from which we get the general study of the aged person, gerontology. Geriatrics is the term applied to medical practice which specializes in the aging. Periodically there are international congresses on gerontology.

This phenomenon has created a new series of questions: What are the processes that produce the typical signs of old age? What happens to the emotional structures of people as they move into old age? How does society treat the aged, and what sociological phenomena do the aged themselves create? How do elderly people pay their bills?

This is an immense problem in the lap of every church but only a pitiful handful realize it, understand it, and do something about it. In some ways churches even aggravate the problems of the aged.

Here are some of those problems:

SECTION 408: THE SENIOR CITIZEN

(1) Our society puts a premium on active people. For example, the church member appreciated the most is the one who will do the most work. The elderly person cannot do very much. He or she encounters what has been called *retirement shock.* This gives the elderly person a sense of uselessness which is psychologically a very destructive feeling.

(2) Our society puts a premium on young people. We have a cult of the youth. The older one gets the less he is part of the crowd, the less he is called upon to do something, and the more risky is his economic status. Pastors face this when they realize that even with their mature experience a congregation will almost uniformly call the younger man rather than the older man. In the life of the church the important offices gyrate toward the younger men and women and away from the older people. This creates feelings of uselessness, helplessness, and self-rejection.

(3) The important people in the church are the "givers." The elderly person lives on an income where he or she is lucky to be able to give anything. During financial campaigns this can give elderly people another set of destructive feelings. Not being a real giver means that they are no longer significant people in a church.

(4) The older a person gets the more he suffers from the "shrinking law." The shrinking law means that a person is called upon for fewer and fewer responsibilities; and due to infirmity there is less and less that he can do. So what he can participate in gets smaller and smaller. His social life progressively shrinks. If the person is not bedridden his activities may still shrink to as little as 5 percent of what they formerly were. But emotions do not necessarily shrink. So with the shrinkage principle slowly reducing a person's participation, his emotional problems do just the reverse—they enlarge.

(5) Elderly and retired people face isolation. They are put in all kinds of rest homes. This means that they live in a very restricted geographical area. More emotional problems are created.

Boredom: What does one do to pass away the time hour by hour in a chair or in a bed or on a bench within the barrier of a rest home?

Loneliness: The universal complaint of elderly people is that they are lonely. True, they see the personnel of the rest home but they don't see relatives, they don't see children, they don't see the events of the day. At least television gives them some escape from the loneliness of their isolation.

167

Exploitation: Many rest homes are pure financial ventures. The help is the poorest possible; the services are greatly limited; and the food barely edible. Elderly people can be subjected to sharp financial practices because they are too old, too tired, too weak, or too confused to cope with this kind of problem.

For those who wish to explore the problem of the aged and Christian ethics in greater detail we suggest Robert Gray and David Moberg's *The Church and the Older Person.*

The local church can do something about the aged in its membership:

(1) It ought to recognize the problem. This sounds odd but it is tragic how few churches do not recognize the problems discussed above when they apply to their very own church members.

(2) It should realize that people age at different rates and make proper accommodations. At age seventy, one person can be very alert and physically active; another person may be intellectually senile and physically feeble. Elderly people cannot be treated on an age basis alone.

(3) It should keep the elderly and the retired in the life of the church as long as the person has the mind and the health to be active.

(4) It should foster healthy attitudes in the church so that elderly people will know that they are understood and appreciated.

(5) If a church has the means it should do something special for the elderly people. A very large church would be wise to have a pastor for the elderly as a tit-for-tat worker for the young people.

(6) Elderly people may become confused about their business matters, health matters, and government matters. Younger people in the church can give them the time, transportation, and help that they need.

(7) Some system of calling on the elderly should be set up in every church. We are not referring here to pastoral calling but to church members visiting the aged. People who are in rest homes or bedridden still need a contact with the rest of the human race. For example, women whose children are married or at school can form small visitation groups that on a weekly or monthly basis engage in the visitation of the elderly. Men may take a Saturday afternoon a month or a late part of Sunday afternoon to do the same kind of calling. But such programs will get underway only as Christian people really feel for the kind of loneliness that plagues elderly people.

(8) Fifty percent of people who are told that their disease is terminal or fatal go into a state of emotional depression. These people are in desperate need of human compassion and concern. Although many institutions have chaplains they are all overworked. The church must feel a special responsibility for such people, and through pastoral and lay visitation the church should minister to these people and give them whatever comfort they can. The concrete expression of genuine concern can make the transition from this world to the next much easier and happier for the terminally sick Christian.

Section 409: The Future of Medicine

Prior to writing this section the author read a series of articles in responsible journals which surveyed medical practices around the world. From this reading two problems were very obvious:

(1) The historical background of medical practice in a country sets the mood for any discussion of the future of medicine within that country. There is no universal or world-wide attitude toward the practice of medicine and there is no world-wide philosophy about medical practice. In England the medical profession has not made a great point about earning a huge income from its profession. Hence, the introduction of socialized medicine did not precipitate a massive objection from the doctors. In America being a doctor has been a direct pathway to becoming a very wealthy person; consequently the slightest suggestions about socialized medicine have met with maximum resistance. This means that in the future there will be several systems of medical practice throughout the world.

(2) It is very difficult to distinguish between ethical problems and practical problems. Is a crowded clinic an administrative problem to which not enough attention has been given or is it an ethical problem revealing the failure of a government to provide an adequate number of doctors? Dozens of such confusing problems arise when one reads medical practices throughout the world. And certainly there is going to be for some time a debate over whether a certain medical problem is a problem of administration or a failure in ethical responsibility.

Our concern in this section is not with traditional problems of medical ethics. For example, the Roman Catholic church has a very articulate system of medical ethics which all Roman Catholic medical personnel are expected to follow. Although Protestants have no such articulate system they have engaged in debates with the Roman Catholic positions as well as having debates among themselves. Our concern is the ethical implications for the future of medicine.

Behind all the theories of medical practice being debated or defended throughout the world there is one common ethical presupposition: *good health and long life are prime human values.* We have come across no discussion where it has been argued that sickness is a virtue and a short life to be desired.

There is no common basis for defending the ethical good or the value of good health. In most cases it is perhaps a veiled *hedonism*: suffering is painful and therefore a lack of good; bodily health produces pleasant feelings and these feelings are part of the basic good of existence. In more articulate works health is defended on humanistic grounds. A healthy body is a basic human value or good. Or it has been argued on religious grounds that the sanctity of life presupposes a healthy body; or in reverse, sickness is a threat to the body and the sanctity of life demands that we have the medical attention necessary to restore the health of the body. If good health and long life were not universally held values then discussions of medical practices and ethics would take some curious turns.

The second most basic observation to be made is that a major illness is beyond the financial ability of most people. Hospitals operate twenty-four hours a day with multiple and complicated staffs. Within the hospital itself are many expensive, specialized services. Medical equipment is becoming more sophisticated and therefore more expensive. The more our medical knowledge grows, the greater is the demand for specialists. Specialists are highly paid people because of the extra nonprofit or low-profit years it takes to become a specialist. The average wage earner does not make enough money, nor could he save enough money, to pay for any kind of extended medical services. Transplants cost from $30,000 to $50,000.

There is one simple and obvious conclusion to the above parargaph: *however it is done the total society alone can pay its medical bills.* At the present time a number of plans are in the experimental stage in all parts of the world ranging from individual compulsory medical insurance to the total medical services provided by the state as in the Soviet Union. It must be seen that they all may be *different* answers, but the *problem* is the same. Stated one way it means that no longer can the average person pay substantial medical bills; and stated another way, it means medical bills can be paid only by the total society. It is not a question *that* this is the case; it is a question now about *how* society pays its own medical bills. That is the real point of controversy.

In reading about medical practices around the world the matters discussed the most and which created the most number of problems were methods of administration. We have already indicated how impossible it is in these instances to determine what is a problem of pure mechanics or administration and what is a possible ethical question.

Here are two examples: (1) *Doctor-patient relationship.* In setting a broken arm any one of twenty doctors can do an adequate job and the doctor-patient relationship is not a crucial item. But in many other diseases the doctor and patient have to work together as a team to learn the right medication, to control medication, to detect progress or relapse, and to provide a certain amount of emotional reenforcement or stabilization. When medicine is part of the program of the state, is it an administrative problem if this relationship is not possible or is it unethical to practice medicine in such a way that the necessary doctor-patient relationship cannot exist? (2) *What is the reward of the doctor?* Here we can take the extremes. The specialist in America is rewarded with a high fee. In Russia a doctor's salary is very average but he enjoys a very high position in society. Is the means by which a doctor is rewarded purely cultural or is there an ethical principle which should determine the kind of reward medical experts should receive?

America and every other advanced culture has the means, or in a few years will have the means, to give every citizen of the country adequate food, adequate clothing, adequate housing, adequate education, adequate employment, and an adequate retirement situation. This is considered more and more the ethical duty of the state in view of modern technology. If a state can provide all these services (and this is no longer debatable), is it not ethically obligated to provide them? Would this not by extension then mean that the state should also provide adequate dental care, medical care, and psychiatric care to its entire citizenry by whatever particular or specific plan it chooses to use?

Section 410: Prison Reform

The New Testament specifies that the visitation of the prisoner is a Christian virtue (Matt. 25:36, Heb. 13:3, 2 Tim. 1:16).

Why should visitation of prisoners be a Christian virtue? First, not all such people are criminals. There are political prisoners who are guilty of no crime but happen to belong to the wrong party. There are ethnic prisoners like Jews, blacks, and Armenians who are in prison not for specific crimes but because of their racial or ethnic origin. There are prisoners who have been jailed because of their religious beliefs. Further, prisoners have always been the subject of brutalities not at all justified by their crime. Finally, even if prisoners are criminals they are persons, and they have as much right to hear the gospel as anybody else.

The early church took this injunction very much to heart. It sent evangelistic teams into the prisons and work camps of the Roman Empire. Such conversions occurred and such revivals took place in the prisons that the Roman government put a stop to the evangelization of prisoners. It has been said that the Christian concern for the criminal based on the Scriptures cited above has done more for the good of the prisoner than anything else in Western civilization. It cannot be denied that some papal decrees have been directed toward the alleviation of the condition of the prisoner. Others have felt that the effect of the church on prison practices has been ever so slight. The church has in fact gone along with the terrible practices that have characterized the treatment of criminals for thousands of years.

Nothing can make a person so emotionally sick and intellectually confused as a study of the history of criminology. What is so terribly embarrassing is that the Christian church has been one of the consenting parties in this sickening story. John Swain documents this fact in *A History of Torture*. Not all who tortured in the name of Christ or the church were really genuine Christian people, but the point remains that the church as the church supported these medieval brutalities. No more wretched institution has been devised by man than the prison, yet man has not been intelligent enough to suggest a *workable* alternative. If war is hell then in its own way prison is two hells.

Brutality has been the one common element that has characterized the prison from ancient civilizations until today. For example, as late as 1630 a doctor received the following penalties for writing a rather ordinary letter of protest to ecclesiastical authorities:

(1) To be whipped in public twice.
(2) To be pilloried.
(3) To have an ear cut off.
(4) To have the nose slit.
(5) To be branded as a Sower of Sedition.
(6) To be fined 10,000 pounds.
(7) To be imprisoned for life.

Has there been any progress since then? Yes, and again, no. One man in the twentieth century was given ten sentences of 199 years each to run consecutively. The "hole" is still common practice in many prisons. A prisoner is put in a very small dark room with only a night shirt for clothing, only the steel floor to sleep on, only bread and water for food with an occasional meal, and no contact with any other human being except the guard who periodically checks to see if the man is still alive. Dipping prisoners in a bathtub filled with ice cold water until they are blue is still part of twentieth-century treatment.

Of course one cannot generalize. Each city, county, and state has its own prison practices. Besides this the federal government has its own prisons with its special practices. The range of practices is very great from methods that are still as brutal and medieval as can be to other practices that try to be as humane as possible.

Real prison reform in modern times is attributed to a book written by John Howard (an Englishman) in 1777 entitled: *The State of Prisons in England and Wales, with Preliminary Observations, and an Account of some Foreign Prisons.* In a most general way it can be said that the very brutal methods of treating prisoners prior to this time have been ended in Western countries. But on the other hand, prison reform is very spotty with many prisons conducting business as usual, and others (such as the California system) trying to be as humane and enlightened as possible in the treatment of criminals.

Very little can be done until the real causes of criminality are known. Just as the real task of medicine is to treat and educate the public to prevent illness rather than cure a person after he is sick, the real task of criminology is to find out what causes crime and try to stop up its origin. At the present time there are three basic theories of what factors make a man a criminal.

(1) *The physiological theory.* Cesare Lombroso of Italy wrote a work in 1876 called *Criminal Man.* In it he defended the thesis that a criminal was born a criminal. He was a person whose physiological composition was such that it drove him to a life of crime.

This theory is not held today as the basic cause for criminality. It is recognized that physiological elements may be factors in criminology. A few psychiatrists believe that alcoholism represents a physiological sensitivity to alcohol and is not therefore psychological in its origin. The blood of the schizophrenic has elements not found in the blood of ordinary people, but here the psychiatrist doesn't know which is the egg and which is the chicken. Do the blood variations produce schizophrenia or does schizophrenia produce the blood variations? Is a psychopath a person who has part of his brain that did not knit together the right way? The belief that homosexuality is essentially rooted in physiological factors still lingers on as a possible explanation of this problem.

(2) *The psychological theory.* It has been argued that all criminal activity is antisocial activity. Antisocial activity is a symptom of a psychological maladjustment to life. Criminals then ought not be sent to prisons but turned over to psychiatrists.

Today no one doubts that psychological disturbances may create criminal careers. Profound disturbances in a child's psychological development do drive the child into crime when he becomes a young adult. It is accepted theory that sexual perversion is the result of very destructive relationships in the child's home. Or orphans, or children of divorced couples, bounced around from institution to institution, or home to home, or relative to relative also often end up as criminals.

(3) *The sociological theory.* Certain segments of society such as ghettos and poverty-stricken areas produce a great number of criminals. Middle-class families as well as wealthy families also produce their particular kind of criminal. Certain kinds of criminal activity can be carried on only by people who are educated. Each level of society has its potential pathological factors that may produce its particular kind of criminal.

There is truth in all three theories. No one theory accounts for all cases. An immense library on criminology has been created as the subject is studied from a dozen different perspectives.

The frustrating element in any study of our prison system is the nest of problems which defy any reasonable solution or the fact that the solution offered is impossible to practice or breaks down in operation.

Here are some concrete examples of this dilemma:

(1) All criminals need some psychological help. Many are in need of extended psychotherapy. What are the problems?

America is short of psychiatrists for its needs in the general population. If there are not enough to go around to the general public, the possibility of a prison system having any kind of real psychiatric help is infinitely remote.

Psychiatrists who do work in prisons are frequently young doctors who want some exposure to the kinds of cases one finds in a penitentiary, but after a year or two they have learned what they came for and leave.

Many of the psychiatric cases in a prison are of the type that offer little prospect of cure or whose cure takes far more time than any psychiatrist can give them. So they go untreated.

Even though we know the immense changes that real psychiatric programs could effect in our prisons, at the present time the situation is almost hopeless.

(2) Segregation of criminals is a must. There should be different kinds of prisons for different kinds of criminals. This is the best way to prevent a prison from being a school for the teaching of crime from inmate to inmate. But when the criminal population grows too fast the criminals have to be put somewhere. This forces the state to put criminals wherever there is space. This means that hundreds of criminals are put into prisons where they don't belong and so the practice of the segregation of criminals collapses.

Another aspect of the same problem is that criminologists have suggested that no prison should have more than 1200 men. With the growing crime rate prisons have had to go way beyond the 1200 limit. The crowding in some penitentiaries defies description. Beds are even lined up in the corridors.

(3) Criminals are to be rehabilitated. Everybody knows this! But how does it work? Supposing a man is taught to be a barber so that when he is released he can earn his living lawfully and be a good citizen. But learning to be a barber, or what else, does not touch whatever factor made the man a criminal in the first place. When he is released he usually becomes a criminal again and not a rehabilitated barber.

But rehabilitation is not only occupational. Therapy groups have been tried as helps for the patient when psychiatric help is not possible. But these have a way of backfiring. The theory and intentions

175

are good, namely, to have the man locate his problem, look it in the face for what it is, see what it does to him, and then try to relearn a constructive way of reacting. But the sessions turn out to be (as far as the mind of the inmate reacts) justifications for the prison sentence, or how better to adjust to prison conditions. The expected psychological healing does not take place.

Or, an inmate is taught to operate a power machine. When released he can find his place in a factory working a power machine and so become a good citizen in his community. However, after fifteen years in prison his ordinary humanity or his ego image is so beaten up, so destroyed, that he can't function in normal society. Certainly he can operate a power machine in a factory but he has to live with people. Years in prison have destroyed his powers to live creatively with people. So he commits another crime and is sent back to prison where once again he feels at home. He is comfortable as a prisoner; he is miserable as a free man in society.

This sort of analysis can go on and on until the mind boggles. For example, those who guard the prisoners live in a prison themselves. They are surrounded by potential psychopathic killers and must conform to prison routine. This can crack them up as well as the criminal. Guards are also threatened. Prisoners warn them that they or their family will be killed or harmed when the prisoner is released.

Then there is the senile prisoner. His life in prison has destroyed his personality. He cannot understand orders and therefore cannot obey them. He is literally shoved through his daily routine by the guards or other prisoners. His incarceration in a prison has become meaningless.

Or consider the cost of building a prison. It is such a specialized building that its cost per square foot is outrageous compared to any other building. Politicians are not easily moved to vote for new prisons because there is no political gain in such a move. The raising of more taxes to pay for a new prison may actually be to the politician's disadvantage. So many prisons are still but one step removed from medieval bastions.

There have been numerous suggestions of prison reform from wardens, sociologists, bar associations, and psychologists. On paper a great number of the abuses can be corrected. But they all get hung up at two points: (i) they cost far more money than either the state can afford or is willing to spend; (ii) they call for specialized personnel who have as yet not been so trained, and even if trained, it is highly questionable that they would want to use their training in the penal system.

This is compounded by the inherent paradox of the prison. It must be an instrument of justice and an institution of redemption at the same time. How to balance these two goals has yet evaded the powers of human intelligence. Or, it must contain at the same time prisoners who yet retain a potential to be a good citizen and prisoners who are hopeless and desperate psychopaths.

What is the Christian concern?

It was indicated at the beginning of this discussion that Scripture itself teaches us compassion for the prisoner. It is therefore a biblical injunction if nothing else. Further, the Christian church is interested in the redemption of men and institutions and not in the destruction of persons and as yet too high a destructive element is in our penal system.

What can the Christian church do?

(1) Members of church families do get into trouble with the law. The pastor should have some understanding of the processes of the law from the time of arrest until a possible sentence to prison. Not all such information is discussed here but many books are available which do give details. Therefore to be an intelligent counselor the pastor should know the minimum facts of criminology.

(2) Some county and city jails permit Sunday services to be conducted for prisoners. Although this may be an open door, the effectiveness of such work is questionable.

(3) Some jails and penitentiaries do have prison chaplains so that the church has some representation in our penal system.

(4) Church councils in cities and towns should make an investigation of the penal system and find out if there are abuses and brutalities or other matters where a more humane treatment of prisoners is called for.

Such councils should also be sensitive about the treatment of prisoners who are members of minority groups to see that they get the same respect from the law as the majority group.

(5) At the more remote level the church should always be in favor of all processes of the state and all laws that have as their goal the more just and humane treatment of prisoners.

177

Section 411: Ethics and Technology of the Future

In the summer of 1965 this author attended an international conference of evangelical Christians in Oxford, England. The composition of the group was essentially scientists in education or in industry. Out of about forty delegates there was one theologian, one Old Testament scholar, one New Testament scholar, and one or two men in philosophy. All the rest were scientists. A sincere effort was made to make the conference international in scope and yet representative of most of the sciences.

The basic purpose of the conference was to assess the present relationship of evangelical Christianity to scientific knowledge in view of the history of science and theology for the past hundred years.

As the discussions progressed through long sessions from early morning to late at night it became apparent that the original issue was not the important one. Discussions about uniformitarian geology or the status of the theory of evolution became secondary to a far more pressing issue. The issue that emerged was how the Christian church was to face the new era of technology that was about to burst on modern society like a tidal wave. The Bible-and-science issue became buried under the enormous theological and ethical problems that would be posed for the church in a super-sophisticated, super-technological society.

The truth of the matter is that if any scholar of one of the major scientific disciplines would just ramble on with the expectations of the achievements of his branch of science in the future, we all would be breathless and stunned at the end of the discussion. The common man has no real sense or understanding of the kind of revolutionary things that are going to take place beginning in the near future.

At different rates of speed the whole world is headed for a technological civilization. In this new technological era present political ideologies will become meaningless. The new technological society will make the capitalism-communism debate meaningless. We shall be neither capitalistic nor communistic but technological. The technological conquest of distances, the ability to share information around the world at electronic speeds, the solving of thousands of traditional problems by electronic methods, the production of goods by cybernetically controlled machines, and the instantaneous processing of data with instantaneous diagnosis or programming will eventually have the effect of making the traditional barriers among nations obsolete.

Computers, cybernetic machines, system controls, and all kinds of electronic gadgetry are all in their infancy. As time proceeds the complexity and sophistication of technology is going to grow at fantastic speeds. Every single phase of human existence is going to undergo radical change. The changes are going to be so radical that in many instances we have no way of making any kind of prediction of the direction in which the development will go. All we know is that we are at the edge of a technological revolution that is beyond our imagination; that this revolution is inevitable; and that it will create patterns of life vastly different from what we now know. Theologically and ethically we sense the dawning of a period which will require the most radical rethinking of the Christian faith ever.

The Christian ethicists who have some idea of these changes to come are convinced that now is the time for the church to start thinking on these matters. One such start is known as *theonetics,* a word composed from the formation of two Greek words which intends to indicate that God ought to control the new technological age. The fear of those concerned with *theonetics* is that the church will not start thinking of the new problems until they actually come and this could well be too little and too late.

We can anticipate two major ethical problems:

(1) *What is the meaning of life in a technological society?* Today the meaning of life which integrates the family and society is the work day of eight to five. This working cycle for both men and women forms the pattern around which all of life is organized and within which most people find the meaning and fulfillment of their lives. The line of production from raw product to finished merchandise sold to the customer, and all the jobs necessary to keep this "production line" going is the essential glue, the essential meaningfulness, of our society.

Technology will disrupt this. Computers, cybernetically controlled machines, and all other sorts of electronic equipment mean that only a few people working a few hours for just a few years will provide all that the world needs in foods and goods. The older meaning of life built essentially on the schema of the Industrial Revolution will have come to an end. The technology of the future will kill it.

If that is the case, what will give meaning or reality to life in a technological world? What holds man together if the present glue of the commercial-industrial-marketing world no longer exists?

But this is only half the story. We are now familiar with organ transplants. What is not so well known is research into shocker drugs or chemicals. Suppose we find out what makes tissue age? Suppose we find a chemical that shocks old tissue back into young tissue? Already the lives of some trees can be perpetuated indefinitely by continuous grafting of new shoots on old limbs. What if we can do this sort of thing to humans? We will then live to a hundred, then a hundred and fifty, and then maybe five hundred years. If we work out the chemistry of aging to the final reaction, and can develop chemicals that will arrest the aging reactions in our tissues, we have become physiologically immortal.

This means that man will have immense periods of time on his hands. What is the meaning to life if a man retires at age thirty? Some unions now want the retirement age reduced to fifty-five. What is the meaning of life if a man retires at age thirty but due to medical science lives to be two hundred years old?

Is the Christian church prepared to answer this question? We are now working on a theology of space. But a theology of time is far more relevant and existentially important. What is the Christian meaning of life for a man who lives to be two hundred years old? This is the kind of question technology will eventually force us to answer. We had better start thinking now for this problem dwarfs into insignificance all the burning social questions of today. The red hot ethical issues of the hour are going to be phased out by advancing technology and the red hot ethical issues for the church of the future are going to come from technology.

(2) The second major ethical issue we can imagine that the technological age will introduce is the question: *how much are we allowed to control human behavior?* Let us put the question another way. If human personality is the most sacred item in our world, to what extent can we change a personality without robbing it of its sacredness or its uniqueness?

Right now modifications of personality can be made chemically. Tranquilizers have tamed the raging maniacs in our mental institutions. This is perhaps the most dramatic sort of thing drugs can currently do to personality. But many other drugs can be used by psychiatrists for many other reasons and each of these drugs is intended to change behavior in one way or another. We know that there certainly must be other drugs as powerful as LSD that can be creatively used to change personality. The possibility of modulating or changing basic human personality by the use of drugs or chemicals is very great. New drugs will come into existence, and more drastic changes will be made.

Psychiatrists can now change personality by electricity. Shock therapy is the most common psychological use of electricity. Already the brains of animals can be penetrated with electrodes so that animals can be depressed or excited through the stimulus of electrical currents. What chemistry might not be able to do, electricity can. It is not inconceivable that electrodes or some other kind of electrical device not yet invented can eliminate all the pathological moods that go with neuroses and psychoses and also create the positive kinds of attitudes that make for healthy minds. The right miniaturized electrode imbedded at exactly the right spot in the brain might eliminate forever the experience of depression.

Where chemistry and electricity may fail there is surgery. The entire brain is being mapped to the smallest degree. Neural circuits are being patiently traced out in the human body. Already some dramatic results have been achieved by destroying a small part of the brain by freezing. Who knows what the brain surgeon of the future will have as tools? Maybe some of the severest symptoms of emotionally disturbed people can be eliminated by one infinitesimal slice in the brain done by some sort of surgical device that replaces the scalpel. Freezing one little connective point in the brain may end many sorts of compulsive behavior.

The changes of personality which could be done chemically, electronically, and surgically are beyond our present calculation. We only know that such changes are possible and that such changes will come. We are back to the problem of the bicycle. The owner keeps changing the parts as they wear out. At what point does the old bicycle cease to exist and the new one come into existence? If human personality is sacred and unique what are the ethical limits in changing it? An organ transplant is one thing, but the radical reconstitution of a human personality is a far different matter. Does the Christian understanding of human personality set a limit to the degree that it can be changed? Is this an ethical problem or a technological problem? Is the transformed person more the real person or more the Christian person than the older sick person? Or must a certain amount of emotional sickness be left in a person as a necessary evil to preserve the original and real person? This is another kind of profound ethical question that the new world of technology will force upon us.

The parallel question is how much can the state control the population by its powers? At the present time the issue centers around the water supply. All sorts of chemicals can be added to the water supply, even birth-control chemicals. As world population goes into the billions and as technology becomes more and more sophisticated, is the bee hive the only model after which human beings can live? Are such controls mandatory in a technological age? Or must the church state what it thinks is the limit of the manipulation by the state on the grounds that to exceed that limit is to turn men into things, people into sociological items, and personalities into its? Let the church explore these matters *now* in order that it might have some sense of orientation when these matters of speculation and science fiction come out of the printed page into the realities of human culture.

BIBLIOGRAPHY

BOOKS AND PAMPHLETS

Aquinas, Thomas. *Summa Theologica.* Translated by Fathers of the English Dominican Province. New York: Benziger, 1947.

Aristophanes. *The Clouds.* Edited by K. J. Dover. New York: Oxford University Press, 1968.

Augustine. *Letters.* Edinburgh: T. P. Clark, 1875.

———. *Reply to Faustus.* Edinburgh: T. P. Clark, 1882.

Ayer, Alfred J. *Language, Truth and Logic.* 2d ed. New York: Dover, 1936.

Barth, Karl. *Against the Stream.* New York: Philosophical Library, 1954.

———. *Church Dogmatics.* Translated by G. T. Thomson. New York: Charles Scribner's, 1936.

———. *Gospel and Law.* Munich: Chr. Kaiser, 1956.

Bennett, John C., et al. *Storm over Ethics.* St. Louis: Bethany Press, 1967.

Bonhoeffer, Dietrich. *Ethics.* London: Fontana Library, 1964.

Broad, C. D. *Five Types of Ethical Theory.* New York: Humanities Press, 1930.

Brunner, H. Emil. *The Divine Imperative.* Philadelphia: Westminster Press, 1947.

Calvin, John. *Institutes of the Christian Religion.* The Library of Christian Classics, vol. 21. Philadelphia: Westminster, 1960.

Camus, Albert. *The Stranger.* New York: Alfred A. Knopf, 1946.

Capps, Walter H., ed. *The Future of Hope.* Philadelphia: Fortress Press, 1970.

Cauthen, Kenneth. *The Impact of American Religious Liberalism.* New York: Harper & Row, 1962.

Childs, Marquis W., and Cater, Douglas. *Ethics in a Business Society.* New York: Mentor Press, 1954.

Cicero. *De Officiis.* Loeb Classical Library, no. 30. Cambridge, Mass.: Harvard University Press, 1930.

Clinebell, Howard, Jr. *Understanding and Counseling the Alcoholic.* Nashville: Abingdon, 1965.

A Community Mental Health Approach to Drug Addiction. Supt. of Documents, U.S. Government Printing Office.

Cox, Harvey, ed. *The Situation Ethics Debate.* Philadelphia: Westminster, 1968.

Edwards, P., ed. *The Encyclopedia of Philosophy.* New York: Macmillan, 1967.

Elert, Werner. *Law and Gospel.* Translated by Edward H. Schroeder. Philadelphia: Fortress Press, 1967.

Eller, Vernard. *The Promise: Ethics in the Kingdom of God.* Garden City: Doubleday, 1970.

Ferm, V., ed. *Encyclopedia of Morals.* New York: Philosophical Library, 1956.

Feuer, Lewis. *The Conflict of Generations.* New York: Basic Books, 1969.

Fletcher, Joseph. *Morals and Medicine.* Boston: Beacon, 1960.

———. *Moral Responsibility.* Philadelphia: Westminster, 1967.

———. "Our Shameful Waste of Human Tissue: An Ethical Problem for the Living and the Dead." In *Religious Situation 1969.* Boston: Beacon Press.

———. *Situation Ethics: The New Morality.* Philadelphia: Westminster, 1966.

Forell, George W., ed. *Christian Social Teachings.* Garden City, N.Y.: Anchor Books, 1966.

———. *Ethics of Decision.* Philadelphia: Fortress Press, 1955.

———. *Faith Active in Love.* Minneapolis: Augsburg, 1960.

Fortas, Abe. *Concerning Dissent and Civil Disobedience.* New York: New American Library, 1968.

Goldberg, B. Z. *The Sacred Fire: The Story of Sex in Religion.* New Hyde Park, N.Y.: University Books, 1958.

Gram, Harold. *The Christian Encounters Ethics and Social Responsibility in Business.* St. Louis: Concordia, 1969.

Gray, Robert M., and Moberg, David O. *The Church and the Older Person.* Grand Rapids, Mich.: Eerdmans, 1962.

Grier, William H., and Cobbs, Price M. *Black Rage.* New York: Basic Books, 1968.

Grotius, Hugo. *The Law of War and Peace.* 1625. Translated by Francis W. Kelsey, et al. Indianapolis, Ind.: Bobbs-Merrill, 1963.

Hall, T. C. *History of Ethics within Organized Christianity.* New York: Charles Scribner's Sons, 1910.

Halverson, Marvin, and Cohen, Arthur A., eds. *A Handbook of Christian Theology.* New York: Meridian Books, 1958.

Hastings, James, ed. *Encyclopedia of Religion and Ethics.* New York: Charles Scribner's Sons, 1913–26.

Henry, Carl F. H., ed. *Aspects of Christian Social Ethics.* Grand Rapids, Mich.: Eerdmans, 1964.

Hesse, Herrmann. *Steppenwolf.* Translated by Basil Creighton. New York: H. Holt & Co., 1929.

Howard, John. *The State of the Prisons.* 1777. New York: Dutton, 1929.

Jolivet, Régis. *Sartre: The Theology of the Absurd.* Paramus, N.J.: Paulist-Newman, 1967.

Kant, Immanuel. "On a Supposed Right To Tell Lies from Benevolent Motives." *Kant's Theory of Ethics.* 5th ed. London: Longman, Greens, 1898.

————. *Religion within the Limits of Reason Alone.* Translated by Theodore M. Greene and Hoyt H. Hudson. 2d ed. La Salle, Ill.: Open Court, 1960.

Kierkegaard, Søren. *The Sickness Unto Death.* Translated by Walter Lowrie. Princeton: Princeton University Press, 1951.

Von Krafft-Ebing, Richard. *Psychopathia Sexualis.* New York: Berkley, 1968.

Ladd, George. *Jesus and the Kingdom.* Waco, Texas: Word Books, 1969.

Lake, Frank. *Clinical Theology.* London: Darton, Longman, & Todd, 1966.

Lehmann, Paul. *Ethics in a Christian Context.* New York: Harper & Row, 1963.

Lombroso, Cesare. *Criminal Man.* New York: G. P. Putnam's Sons, 1911.

Long, Edward Le Roy, Jr. *Conscience and Compromise: An Approach to Protestant Casuistry.* Philadelphia: Westminster, 1954.

Low, Abraham. *Mental Health Through Will-Training.* Boston: Christopher, 1968.

Luther, Martin. *Luther's Larger Catechism*. Translated by J. M. Lenker. Minneapolis, Minn.: Augsburg, 1967.

———. "Ob Kriegesleute auch in seligem Stande sein Konnen" [Whether soldiers too can be saved]. *Philadelphia Edition of Luther's Works,* vol. 5. Philadelphia: Muhlenberg Press, 1943.

———. *Three Treatises.* Philadelphia: Muhlenberg Press, 1947.

McArthur, Harvey K. *Understanding the Sermon on the Mount.* New York: Harper's, 1960.

Macquarrie, John. *Dictionary of Christian Ethics.* Philadelphia: Westminster, 1967.

Miller, Arthur. *The Death of a Salesman.* New York: Viking Press, 1949.

Moltmann, Jürgen. *Religion, Revolution and the Future.* New York: Charles Scribner's, 1969.

Niebuhr, Reinhold. *An Interpretation of Christian Ethics.* New York: Harper & Bros., 1935.

———. *Moral Man and Immoral Society.* New York: Charles Scribner's, 1932.

Nietzche, Friedrich. *The Antichrist.* New York: Alfred A. Knopf, 1920.

Nygren, Anders. *Agape and Eros.* New York: Harper & Row, 1969.

Oden, Thomas C. *Radical Obedience: The Ethics of Rudolph Bultmann.* Philadelphia: Westminster, 1964.

Pascal, Blaise. *Provincial Letters.* Translated by A. J. Krailsheimer. New Orleans: Pelican, 1968.

Pierce, Claude A. *Conscience in the New Testament.* Naperville, Ill.: Allenson, 1955.

Plato. *The Euthyphro.* Translated by Benjamin Jowett. New York: Tudor, n.d.

Psychedelics and the College Student. Princeton, N.J.: Princeton University Press.

Ramsey, Ian T. *Christian Ethics and Contemporary Philosophy.* New York: Macmillan, 1966.

Ramsey, Paul. "On Updating Death." In *Religious Situation 1969.* Boston: Beacon Press.

Rauschenbusch, Walter. *Christianizing the Social Order.* New York: Macmillan, 1915.

———. *A Theology for the Social Gospel.* New York: Abingdon, 1917.

Reichenbach, Hans. *The Rise of Scientific Philosophy*. Berkeley, Cal.: University of California Press, 1951.

Roberti, F. Cardinal. *Dictionary of Moral Theology*. Westminster, Md.: Newman, 1962.

Robinson, J. A. *Honest to God*. Philadelphia: Westminster, 1963.

Schrey, Heinz-Horst; Walz, Hans Herman; and Whitehouse, W. A. *The Biblical Doctrine of Justice and Law*. Naperville, Ill.: Allenson, 1955.

Scott, James Brown. *The Spanish Origin of International Law*. London: H. Milford, 1934.

Seligman, Edward R. A., ed. *Encyclopedia of the Social Sciences*. 15 vols. New York: Macmillan, 1930–35.

Sidgwick, Henry. *Methods of Ethics*. Edited by E. Constance Jones. 7th rev. ed. Chicago: University of Chicago Press, 1962.

Simmons, Jerry L., and Winograd, B. *It's Happening*. Santa Barbara, Cal.: McNally, 1966.

Sinclair, Upton. *The Jungle*. New York: Harper's, 1951.

Stamm, J. J., and Andrew, M. E. *The Ten Commandments in Recent Research*. Naperville, Ill.: Allenson, 1967.

Swain, John. *A History of Torture*. New York: Award Books, 1969.

Terhune, William T., M.D. *The Safe Way to Drink: How To Prevent Alcohol Problems Before They Start*. New York: Morrow, 1968.

Thielecke, Helmut. *Theological Ethics*. Philadelphia: Fortress, 1966–69.

Till, Anthony. *What You Should Know Before You Buy a Car*. Los Angeles: Sherbourne Press, 1968.

Tillich, Paul. *Love, Power, and Justice*. Magnolia, Mass.: Peter Smith, 1960.

————. *Systematic Theology*. 3 vols. New York: Harper's, 1967.

Troeltsch, Ernst. *The Social Teachings of the Christian Churches*. New York: Macmillan, 1931.

Tsanoff, R. A. *The Moral Ideals of Our Civilization*. New York: E. P. Dutton, 1942.

Walker, B. R. *The New Immorality*. New York: Doubleday, 1968.

Warnock, Mary. *Ethics Since 1900*. New York: Oxford University Press, 1968.

————. *Existentialist Ethics*. New York: St. Martin's Press, 1967.

Watson, John. *Behavior: An Introduction to Comparative Psychology*. (1914) New York: Holt, Rinehart, & Winston, 1967.

Webb, Charles. *The Graduate.* New York: New American Library, 1964.

Westermarck, E. *Christianity and Morals.* Freeport, N.Y.: Books for Libraries, 1969.

Xenophon. *The Memorabilia.* Cambridge: Harvard University Press, 1938.

PERIODICALS

Awake, 22 August 1969, pp. 17–23.

Center Magazine. Center for the Study of Democratic Institutions. Santa Barbara, Cal.

Christian Century, 15 October 1969, p. 1310.

Fletcher, Joseph. "Six Propositions: The New Look in Christian Ethics." *Harvard Divinity Bulletin* 4 (1959) :1–18.

Handy. "The Social Gospel in Historical Perspective." *Andover Newton Quarterly* 9 (1969) :171.

"The Hippies—1968." *Religion in Life* 38 (1968) :498–525.

Soulen, Richard S. "Marriage and Divorce: A Problem in New Testament Interpretation." *Interpretation* 23 (1969) :439–50.

Time, 31 October 1969.